50 Festive Ideas for Evangelistic Events

MARK AND EMMA GREENWOOD

EASTBOURNE

Contents

Foreword 9
Preface 11
Acknowledgements 13
Introduction 15
How to Use This Book 17

Burns Night **25**
1. Burns Night Event 27
2. Burns Night Victuals 33
3. Talk: 'Burns Night' 34

Valentine's Day **37**
4. Talk: 'How to Have a Healthy Relationship' 39
5. Mr & Mrs 42

Shrove Tuesday **47**
6. Mardi Gras Masquerade Ball 49
7. Talk: 'The Message of Mardi Gras' 51
8. Pancake Olympics 54
9. Pancake Puzzle 55
10. Talk: 'Don't Put All Your Eggs in One Pancake' 57
11. Shrove Tuesday Traditional Recipes 60

Commonwealth Day/International Evening   **65**
12. Talk: 'What Is Jesus For?'   67
13. Interview a Christian of a Different Nationality 70
14. Decorations, Music and Food from Around
    the World   71

St Patrick's Day/Irish Night   **73**
15. Talk: 'To Be Sure, To Be Sure'   75
16. Irish Quiz   78
17. Traditional Irish Recipes   81

Mother's Day   **85**
18. Talk: 'Some Mothers Do 'Ave 'Em'   87
19. Short Play: 'The Prodigal Daughter'   90
20. A Gift for Mum   95

Easter   **97**
21. Talk: 'Happy Easter'   99
22. Puppet Show: 'Hot Cross Herbie'   102
23. Art and Craft Gallery   117

Father's Day   **119**
24. Talk: 'God's Conveyor Belt'   121
25. The Generation Game   124

Football Final/Sports Event   **133**
26. Big Screen Event   135
27. Talk: 'Football and the Game of Life'   136
28. Awards Ceremony and Meal for Football Team   139
29. Football Five-a-Side Tournament   140
30. Talk: 'The Greatest Commentator'   141

Summer Holiday   **145**
31. Talk: 'Stop! Are You on the Right Track?'   147
32. Treasure Hunt Car Rally   149

CONTENTS

Harvest   **153**
33. Talk: 'A Time for Giving'   155
34. Harvest Festival Collection 'Jewish Style'   158

All Saints' Day (Alternative Halloween)   **161**
35. Talk: 'Trick or Treat?'   163
36. Seasonal Games   166
37. Quiz   170

Bonfire Night   **173**
38. Talk: 'Remember, Remember, the Fifth of November!'   175
39. Talk: 'Say It with Fireworks'   178
40. Firework/Bonfire Party   181
41. Recipes   185

Remembrance Sunday   **189**
42. Talk: 'A Day to Remember'   191
43. Remembrance Sunday Service   194

Christmas   **197**
44. Talk: 'The Problem with Christmas'   199
45. Christmas Meal   202
46. Christmas Craft   205
47. Talk: 'A Christmas Carol'   207
48. Christmas Presentation: 'Scrooge'   210
49. The Carol Service   236
50. Puppet Show: 'Stable Relationships'   241

Foreword

I am delighted to commend *50 Festive Ideas for Evangelistic Events*. Originality is often an unexplored territory. Mark and Emma Greenwood have blazed a new trail, putting creativity to work by looking at the same thing as everyone else and then thinking something different.

The message of Christianity is good news, but many people are not hearing it. How can it be packaged and presented in a way people can understand? Here are fifty ways to start with! Mark and Emma have done a superb job in helping us to communicate the unchanging message of Jesus Christ relevantly at different times of the year.

In my work as an evangelist I have visited hundreds of churches on five continents, and I have found time and again that if you refuse to accept anything but the best, you get the best more often! These ideas are truly excellent, and I hope that as you use them you will sow into the lives of many people seed that will produce good fruit. An idea is a funny little thing that won't work unless you do! Don't just entertain new ideas – put them to work.

I think we are often faced with great opportunities disguised as impossible situations. Opportunity knocks, but it has never been known to turn the knob and walk in. When the window of opportunity appears, don't pull down the shade. We are reminded in the Bible in Ecclesiastes 3 verse 1,

'There is a time for everything, a season for every activity under heaven.' Festive events are great opportunities to communicate the truth about Jesus Christ. There is indeed a right time for everything in this book.

J. John

Preface

I was once in a school staff room when I read this notice: 'I know that you think you know what you thought you said, but I'm not sure that what you thought you said is what I actually heard.' In other words communication is not easy!

Jesus used stories the people understood to communicate something they didn't understand. In my last fifteen years of working in full-time evangelism, I have always tried to use a similar method. How can I package the gospel message? How can I help churches to put on events that people will be happy to come to and be happy afterwards that they went? If people aren't ready to make a commitment to God, but we've sent them away from the event with their perceptions about Christians changed *and* having learned what the message of Christianity really is, then we have done a good job.

In this book, Emma and I have tried to help you, the reader, put on good evangelistic events with the minimum of organizational effort. We have provided you with ready-made ideas, talks and publicity. If we can inspire you to put on successful outward-looking events by doing some of the hard work for you, then this book was well worth the effort. I hope it inspires you to write lots of programmes yourselves. Who knows, maybe you might write the next book!

Mark Greenwood

11

Note: Mark is Director and Evangelist with the Goings Trust, a Christian organization that is dedicated to the relevant biblical communication of the Christian message. Contact Mark and Emma at the Goings Trust, P.O. Box 350, Huddersfield HD2 2YB, or email them at goingstrust@ntlworld.com.

Acknowledgements

I am always grateful for the many people who encourage me in my ministry. Thanks to Emma, who took on the co-authorship of this book and by doing so encouraged me to write it – I wouldn't have done it without her. Thanks to my dear friend J. John, who has helped me immensely in my ministry, not least in introducing me to Kingsway, as well as the other opportunities he has given. Thank you, Richard Herkes and Kingsway, for being willing to work with me in getting my first book published.

Thanks go to my close friend Joseph Boot, who encouraged me to run with the book. I would like to thank the Reverend Bob McDonald and the Gateway Church in Bradford and Peter Hannam of the Elim Pentecostal Church in Huddersfield, who were willing to try out some of the events and talks in this book when they hadn't been done before. Thanks to Kath Froud for proofreading the talks. Thanks also to Neil Simpson and David Simpkin for contributing the puppet scripts, Sarah Hicks and Noel Donaldson for helping with the drama scripts and David Leek for the artwork.

A final thanks to OAC ministries, who taught me and released me into preaching evangelism. It is their training that has formed the bedrock of the way I communicate the Christian message today.

Introduction

There are certain times of the year when people warm more to the idea of coming to church. Christmas, obviously, and to an extent Easter too, as well as weddings, funerals and christenings. In the past the events of the church calendar played an important part in people's lives and the passing of the seasons was celebrated within a Christian context. In our haste to update the church and become relevant to new generations, many of us have decided to sweep aside the celebrations of the passing year as irrelevant. What we haven't seemed to realise is that 'the world' still celebrates seasonal events with great enthusiasm, while we have a year that passes from Sunday to Sunday, much the same.

This book encourages you to revive discarded seasonal occasions and to add some new ones too! You will find that evangelistic events are much easier to promote to those outside the church if based around familiar festivals, and at the same time you will be surprised how much you and your church enjoy celebrating God's seasons together.

The fifty ideas and talks in the book are organized under fifteen headings, one heading for each well-known seasonal occasion in the year. Each idea or talk can be used on its own as part of an already planned service or event. Alternatively, the ideas supplied under each heading can be used together as an entire programme for an outreach event or evangelistic church service. Many of the events would suit house-group as well as 'full-church' gatherings – just scale down the approach as appropriate.

In addition, this book can be used to provide a long-term evangelistic strategy for your church or house group. The seasonal outreach events could run as an evangelistic programme over a couple of years. This way those you are trying to reach will become aware that your church holds events to celebrate the passing year together and will anticipate the next event and invitation.

Some sections of the book provide suggestions for more than one event per seasonal occasion (e.g. Easter and Christmas), or a choice of talks. Also, some event ideas would be appropriate at any time of the year (e.g. the International Evening suggested for Commonwealth Day or the Irish Night suggested for St Patrick's Day).

How to Use This Book

This section outlines some hints and tips to help with the smooth running of the events suggested. We pass these ideas on to you from our experience of running similar events in churches of all denominations.

Planning your events

First ask yourself a number of questions:

What is the aim of the event?

Try to think in a long-term strategic manner rather than hold sporadic, unconnected one-off evangelistic events. Don't try to host all the events suggested in this book in one year, but allow the book to help you plan over the next two or even three years. Not all events have to demonstrably preach the gospel – you may wish to make some of the events lower key. If this is your plan, host the lower-key events first, as they are useful if you want to build long-term relationships with people. In these 'low-key' events it may be better not to have a speaker at all, or just to give a short talk. However, it is helpful, even in 'no talk' events, to say something at the end, even if it is simply along the lines of, 'Thank you for coming today. We would love to see you again some time. If we can be of any assistance to you, please let us know.' When choosing the type of event remember to choose something that will work in your church, your neighbourhood and your circumstances.

Will you charge for the event?

We have found that usually the church member inviting guests will pay for the tickets. Whether you decide to charge or not, it is best to ticket the event. It gives the visitor a greater sense of obligation and it helps with any catering arrangements, giving you a better idea of how many people will be attending. In our experience ticketed events tend to attract more people rather than fewer, even at those events where the visitor has had to pay for the ticket themselves!

Where will you hold your event?

There is a lot to be said for holding events in secular venues. There are many reasons for this: it's a neutral venue, so people may relax more; there can sometimes be a better ambience; if the event is held in a pub the regulars could be invited and may well look in anyway. Sometimes, however, a non-church venue can work against you. It may prove difficult to get visitors into a church building later (if they attend an event held in the church buildings they have already jumped one hurdle) and sometimes the noise of secular venues (e.g. pubs) can be a problem, especially if music is playing in the public bar, as you have no control over it. Also the times at which you can have access to the venue may be restricted and this may cause problems setting up and tidying away at the end. With regard to the venue, the question to ask yourself with each event is, 'What am I trying to accomplish and which venue best facilitates that?'

Profile and publicity

Put posters up in the church buildings, but also think about appropriate places in your community where you can display them. You will find that some shops, post offices, community centres and doctors' surgeries will allow you to advertise local events. Ask members of the church to put posters in their house windows. This works particularly well in the local church community.

Some events will work well when focused simply on inviting friends and family; others may benefit from a leaflet drop through letterboxes in the local community. If people see the publicity at different places, a higher profile is created. If possible distribute flyers mid-morning, as people are more likely to read something that is among their post; junk mail often arrives later in the day.

It would be a good idea to create a special church display for use at evangelistic events. Don't just use your normal church noticeboard. Create an attractive bright free-standing display that can be used outside as well as inside. You should have details about the weekly events your church holds (e.g. church services, mums and tots, youth groups, luncheon club) and posters for any planned future events. Have pockets containing free literature and flyers about your church and events (e.g. Alpha) that people can take away.

Prayer

Prayer is immensely important when it comes to asking people to events; it is often the deciding factor, building confidence in the 'asker' and getting a positive response from the 'asked'. Bearing this in mind, ask yourself, 'How will we pray for the people we want to come?'

We use a simple but effective prayer strategy to get church members praying and motivated about inviting their friends to events.

Step one

Distribute a simple form and ask everyone in your church to submit a list of up to ten people they would like to invite to an event (they can give first names only if they want confidentiality). Collect the forms and compile the names into a directory. Distribute a directory to each person in the church. The aim is that everyone in the church prays for each person in the directory once a month. In a church of fifty people each person gets prayed for fifty times in the month. As part of a long-term evangelism strategy, that's 600 times in a year!

Step two

As the event gets nearer, implement the four-week prayer strategy. Produce the following points on overheads and launch them at consecutive Sunday services, encouraging the whole church to participate.

- *Week 1:* Ask God whom you should invite. When God shows you, pray for them for this week but don't invite them yet. Ask God if there are any more people you should invite.
- *Week 2:* Ask God for the right opportunity. Ask God how you should invite them. For example, should you go for a meal or a drink, or just ask them straight out? Pray for them to make a commitment to God. Don't invite them yet.
- *Week 3:* Pray they say 'yes' and invite them this week. Ask God to give you confidence. Remember how God said you should invite them. Give them an invitation card.
- *Week 4:* Pray they make a commitment. Pray that they would come to the event. Make final arrangements to meet with them.

Each point becomes a prayer focus for church members for the week. The points could be discussed and prayed through in home groups and cell groups. You could provide handouts detailing the point for the week, to be distributed after the service.

Encourage church members to actually accompany their friends to the event. It's awkward for people to come to anything that's new. Don't simply expect guests to turn up. Sometimes it helps to arrange to meet guests beforehand, maybe to go out somewhere beforehand and make an evening of it.

Event timings

Be aware that people often arrive late. A good way to deal with this is to have some music playing and serve drinks and nibbles for the first fifteen minutes or so of the evening. You may want to ask a few church members to look out for people who are by themselves.

If you are going to have a talk at the end of the event make sure a realistic amount of time is left so that you can say what you want to say without being rushed. However, generally the talk is best given about three-quarters of the way through an event. When planning the event timings, allow time for tea, coffee and biscuits at the end; this provides flexibility in the programme and also gives time for chat among visitors and those who invited them.

Finally, it's a good idea to briefly outline the programme for the evening at the start, to alleviate any nerves and apprehension about what is going to take place.

How to use the talks

Allow approximately fifteen to twenty minutes per talk. The talks use a lot of illustration. We feel, following Jesus' example, that the use of illustration and storytelling is of utmost importance when preaching evangelistically. Mark always uses this motto when he prepares his talks: 'A point for the head, a story for the heart and a scripture for the soul.'

The talks take the following format.

The gospel points

We have indicated the aim of each sermon point so that you know what should be emphasized about the gospel at that time. Most of the talks are in three points. We include a verse from the Bible for each point; these are key to the effectiveness of a gospel message, as they back up what is being asserted with Scripture. Do feel free to use your own translations, but make sure that all Christian words that you quote from the Bible are explained as they are used. Religious words can be confusing at best and intimidating at worst.

The three-point gospel message we use can be briefly summarized thus:

1. Sin and separation
2. Forgiveness, cross and resurrection
3. Response

Response

You may feel it inappropriate to end a talk at a social event with a call to commitment. However, we have found that as long as this is handled sensitively and not strung out, visitors are not embarrassed and do not mind. We have also found that most of the time someone does make a response to God and we have been glad that we did not miss the opportunity by being overly seeker-sensitive.

A good way to finish each talk is to repeat the 'A, B, C' at the end like this:

'So what about you? Would you like to say to God . . .

- I *admit* to you and myself that I have sinned and left you out of my life and gone my own way
- I *believe* that Jesus came to this world to die on the cross to take my punishment so that I could be forgiven
- I *commit* my whole life to you and turn away from living life my way to start living it your way?

'If you would like to pray that to God, then you can say "Yes!" to God even now in your own heart. God will hear it and if you mean it he will forgive you. If that's how you're feeling, just say "Yes" to God now, in the quietness of your own heart and mind.'

It helps to have some mechanism to identify those who have responded, so that you can get some helpful literature to them and arrange for a follow-up meeting if they want one. There are a number of ways of doing this:

1. At the end of the event ask people to fill in a response card as they leave. The cards could have four tickable options:

    - I have previously said 'Yes' to God
    - I said 'Yes' to God tonight
    - I would like to find out more about the Christian faith
    - I would like an invitation to a similar event

    Also include a space for their name and address and the name of the person who invited them to the event. Make sure you provide pens.

2. The speaker or a dedicated person can stand with leaflets near the door as people leave. At the end of the talk introduce the person and explain that they have some

booklets for anyone who said 'Yes' to God tonight and would like to find out more. Explain that if they would prefer, they can speak to whoever they came with and ask them to get the booklets for them.

3. They could simply be encouraged to tell the people they came with.

Post-event

Make sure that you promptly follow up any requests for information or help following the event. Don't forget to send invitations for the next event to those who requested them.

Evaluate your event and think about how you could make the next one even better. You could even form an event committee to meet afterwards to discuss ideas and offer constructive criticism.

Burns Night

Introduction

Burns Night is celebrated in honour of Robert Burns on 25th January every year, the date of this famous Scottish poet's birthday. Although traditionally a Scottish festival, Burns Night is celebrated all over the world and there are over 2,000 Burns Clubs globally. Burns Night celebrations can range from a formal gathering of academics to an *ad hoc* student party. Although the outline given here is for a relatively formal Burns Night celebration, it would be perfectly viable just to invite a few friends round or have a social evening in your house/cell group. The only essential ingredients of a Burns Night celebration are the 'chairman' (to give a short address), the 'celebrants' (guests) and the 'victuals' (haggis, etc.) and of course the recital of some Rabbie Burns poetry!

1. Burns Night Event

The traditional elements of a Burns Night celebration are Scottish fare, songs, poems, music, readings and a short address. Following is a suggested evening plan and menu, with further details concerning food outlined in Idea 2. It is a good idea to provide a programme card for the evening, which can be displayed at each table. Robert Burns poetry audio compilations exist if you do not have access to a Scottish person who can help with the pronunciation of the poetry.

Welcome and grace

The guests are welcomed by the host and invited to enjoy themselves and relax. The host then recites the traditional Scottish 'Selkirk Grace':

> Some hae meat and cannot eat,
> Some cannot eat that want it,
> But we hae meat and we can eat,
> Sae let the Lord be thankit.
> Amen.

Starter

Cock-a-leekie soup.

Parade of the haggis

The guests all stand and the haggis is brought to the top table on a platter by the chef to the sound of bagpipes and the clapping of the guests. (If you do not know a piper who can lead the haggis in, then a recording will suffice.) The host then recites the famous Robbie Burns poem 'Address to a Haggis'. When the line 'an' cut you up wi' ready sleight' is recited, the host should cut open the haggis with a knife. When the poem is finished it is traditional for the guests to clap and toast the haggis with a 'wee dram' of Scotch whisky.

Address to a Haggis

> Fair fa' your honest, sonsie face,
> Great chieftain o' the pudding-race!
> Aboon them a' ye tak your place,
> Painch, tripe, or thairm:
> Weel are ye wordy o'a grace
> As lang's my arm.
>
> The groaning trencher there ye fill,
> Your hurdies like a distant hill,
> Your pin wad help to mend a mill
> In time o' need,
> While thro' your pores the dews distil
> Like amber bead.
>
> His knife see rustic Labour dight,
> An' cut you up wi' ready sleight,
> Trenching your gushing entrails bright,
> Like ony ditch;
> And then, O what a glorious sight,
> Warm-reekin', rich!
>
> Then, horn for horn, they stretch an' strive:
> Deil tak the hindmost! on they drive,
> Till a' their weel-swall'd kytes belyve

Are bent like drums;
Then auld Guidman, maist like to rive,
Bethankit! hums.

Is there that owre his French ragout
Or olio that wad staw a sow,
Or fricassee wad make her spew
Wi' perfect sconner,
Looks down wi' sneering, scornfu' view
On sic a dinner?

Poor devil! see him owre his trash,
As feckless as wither'd rash,
His spindle shank, a guid whip-lash;
His nieve a nit;
Thro' bluidy flood or field to dash,
O how unfit!

But mark the Rustic, haggis-fed,
The trembling earth resounds his tread.
Clap in his walie nieve a blade,
He'll mak it whissle;
An' legs an' arms, an' hands will sned,
Like taps o' trissle.

Ye Pow'rs, wha mak mankind your care,
And dish them out their bill o' fare,
Auld Scotland wants nae skinking ware
That jaups in luggies;
But, if ye wish her gratefu' prayer
Gie her a haggis!

Main course

Haggis with bashed neeps and tatties.

Address

A short address will not seem out of place, as it is traditional
to have a speaker at a Burns Night. Use the evangelistic talk
provided in this section; alternatively ask a Scot to give their
testimony (even better if they arrive in a kilt!).

Dessert

Typsy laird (sherry trifle), followed by coffee.

Recitals

Singing is a traditional element of a Burns Night. The hymn
'I Cannot Tell' (by W. Y. Fullerton) sung to the tune of 'O
Danny Boy' has a Celtic feel. Provide the words and encour-
age the guests to sing along.

Ask a number of people to prepare readings of poetry
beforehand. The following are well known or suitable Burns
pieces.

A Red, Red Rose

O my Luve's like a red, red rose,
That's newly sprung in June:
O my Luve's like the melodie,
That's sweetly play'd in tune.

As fair art thou, my bonnie lass,
So deep in luve am I;
And I will luve thee still, my dear,
Till a' the seas gang dry.

Till a' the seas gang dry, my dear,
And the rocks melt wi' the sun;
And I will luve thee still, my dear,
While the sands o' life shall run.

And fare-thee-weel, my only Luve!
And fare-thee-weel, a while!
And I will come again, my Luve,
Tho' 'twere ten thousand mile!

Paraphrase of the First Psalm

The man, in life wherever plac'd,
Hath happiness in store,
Who walks not in the wicked's way,
Nor learns their guilty lore!

Nor from the seat of scornful pride
Casts forth his eyes abroad,
But with humility and awe
Still walks before his God.

That man shall flourish like the trees,
Which by the streamlets grow;
The fruitful top is spread on high,
And firm the root below.

But he whose blossom buds in guilt
Shall to the ground be cast,
And, like the rootless stubble, tost
Before the sweeping blast.

For why? that God the good adore,
Hath giv'n them peace and rest,
But hath decreed that wicked men
Shall ne'er be truly blest.

Although you should be sure to include some Burns poetry, a Burns Night can also include other readings or songs with a Scottish flavour, or indeed compositions by the guests themselves. A Burns Night is an event where guests are encouraged to take an active part, hence you should have a number of poems printed out for people to recite should they wish to join in.

Auld Lang Syne

'Auld Lang Syne' was written by Robert Burns and the evening should conclude with this recital. Everyone should stand and link arms in the traditional manner and join in with the chorus, but the verses are not well known, so ask someone with a good, strong voice to prepare beforehand.

Should auld acquaintance be forgot,
And never brought to mind?
Should auld acquaintance be forgot,
And auld lang syne!

*Chorus: For auld lang syne, my dear,
            For auld lang syne.
            We'll tak a cup o' kindness yet,
            For auld lang syne.*

And surely ye'll be your pint stowp!
And surely I'll be mine!
And we'll tak a cup o' kindness yet,
For auld lang syne.

We twa hae run about the braes,
And pou'd the gowans fine;
But we've wander'd mony a weary fit,
Sin' auld lang syne.

We twa hae paidl'd in the burn,
Frae morning sun till dine;
But seas between us braid hae roar'd
Sin' auld lang syne.

And there's a hand, my trusty fere!
And gie's a hand o' thine!
And we'll tak a right gude-willie waught,
For auld lang syne.

2. Burns Night Victuals

The traditional fare for Burns Night is haggis, bashed neeps and tatties, accompanied by Scotch whisky. Haggis can be bought from most large well-stocked supermarkets. Neeps are more commonly known as turnips or swedes. Peel, dice and boil until soft and then mash with butter, salt and pepper. 'Tatties', or potatoes, should also be peeled, boiled and mashed with butter.

The menu outlined in Idea 1 suggests cock-a-leekie soup to start the meal and typsy laird trifle for dessert. Cock-a-leekie and other traditional Scottish soups can be bought canned by Baxters. Typsy laird is merely a traditional sherry trifle. A 'wee dram' of Scotch whisky could be served after the soup for toasting the haggis, but make sure you provide a non-alcoholic option as well.

3. Talk: 'Burns Night'

Opening illustration

Get everyone to sing 'Auld Lang Syne' as we sing it today.

Few of us escape hearing this song sung over New Year. We only sing the first and last verses these days, but Burns' poem written in 1794 has five verses, although there is some argument as to the correct order. It's a song of friendship and salutation recognized across the English-speaking world.

Point 1 (sin): He was looking back to what he had

Robbie Burns' life was not the best of lives. He was someone who always enjoyed a good drink – in fact his drinking hastened his own death. But in this song he was more concerned with being drunk with the happiness of sharing memories with a childhood friend.

Verse 1: Should we forget our old friends, and never think of them again? Should we forget our old friends, and the days long past?

Verse 3: We two have run about the hills, And picked the daisies fine; But we've wandered far away from there, Since the days of long ago.

Verse 4: We two have paddled in the stream from dawn till dinner time; But broad seas have roared between us, Since those days of long ago.

He looked back to the friendship he once had with a particular person, but was sad that he no longer had it.

(Bible verse: Isaiah 59:2) Your sins have hidden his face from you.

God made us to have a friendship with him. But just as broad seas of time had roared between Burns and his childhood friend, so a divide has come between us and God. Our sins, the things we do against God, have stopped us knowing God in our lives.

> Verse 5: And there's a hand, my trusty brother! And give me a hand of yours!

God wants us to walk hand in hand with him. He made us to share life with him, but we have decided that we want to live life without him. How sad it is that we don't enjoy what God has for us.

Point 2 (forgiveness): Looking forward to the future

Robbie Burns' poem 'To a Mouse' says, 'The best laid schemes of mice and men often go astray.' He was ploughing his field when he ran over a mouse's home.

(Bible verse: Jeremiah 29:11) 'For I know the plans I have for you,' declares the Lord, 'plans to prosper you and not to harm you, plans to give you hope and a future.'

We plan our lives the best we can, but how often do our plans not work out? God wants us to live our lives according to his plan because he knows that our lives will then be successful. God's plan for our lives will never go astray.

God planned right from the beginning of time that Jesus

would die on a cross so that we could be forgiven. He planned that Jesus would rise again from the dead and that's exactly what he did. Nothing would cause this plan to go astray.

Point 3 (response): Looking back and looking forward

At this time of year we make New Year's resolutions. We see a chance to put the past to bed and look forward to a new start. God wants us to change our lives. The difference is that he gives us the power to make those changes.

- Admit to God and yourself that you have sinned; that you have left God out of your life and gone your own way.
- Believe that Jesus came to this world to die on the cross to take your punishment so that you can be forgiven.
- Commit your whole life to God. Turn away from living life your way and start living it God's way.

Do this and mean it, and God will forgive you.

Valentine's Day

Introduction

February 14th is not the best night to hold a church event, as many couples will be celebrating Valentine's Day together privately. Hold a Valentine's event in the days leading up to or immediately following the 14th February. Most couples with children do not get the chance to go out together frequently, so offer a free babysitting service to those who wish to come to the event.

4. Talk: 'How to Have a Healthy Relationship'

Opening illustration

It has been suggested humorously by a woman that the following are the best rules for relationships between couples:

1. The female makes all the rules.
2. The rules are subject to change at any time without prior notification.
3. No male can possibly know all the rules.
4. If the female suspects that the male knows the rules, she must immediately change some or even all of the rules.
5. The female is NEVER wrong.
6. If the female is wrong, it is due to a gross misunderstanding on the part of the male.
7. If the previous rule applies, the male must apologize immediately for causing the misunderstanding.
8. The female may change her mind at any given point.
9. The male must never change his mind without written consent from the female.
10. The male must remain calm at all times, unless the female wants him to be angry or upset.
11. The female must under no circumstances let the male know whether or not she wants him to be angry or upset.
12. The female has every right to be angry or upset at any time.

There is a way to behave in order to get on with someone. It is a two-way thing and not just one individual's ideas.

Here are three pointers to help us have a healthy relationship.

Point 1 (sin): Putting each other first

Imagine your partner came up to you and said, 'I love you with half of my heart.' It is estimated that three out of five marriages end in divorce. This is due to the fact that people stop putting each other first. The way to have a healthy relationship is to put each other first. In our world we don't have a relationship with God because we don't put him first.

(Bible verse: Matthew 22:37) Love the Lord your God with all your heart and with all your soul and with all your mind.

God wants us to put him in first place. Sin is not putting God in first place.

Point 2 (forgiveness): Forgiving wrong

Someone once said, 'An ideal marriage is a deaf husband and a blind wife.' It's not true, of course. We should see and hear each other's failures and forgive them. God saw our failures and forgave us. The way to have a healthy relationship with each other is to forgive wrong.

(Bible verse: Romans 5:8) While we were sinners, Christ died for us.

Christ died on the cross for us, taking the punishment for our wrong.

Point 3 (response): Accepting blame

A brave (or maybe foolish) man once said, 'Every man needs a wife, because there are many things he cannot blame on the government.' We are always too ready to blame people for our errors. For example, when a husband can't find something, the first thing he does is blame his wife. Never overlook what may be your fault; never forget that you can take some responsibility.

The way to have a healthy relationship with each other is to accept blame. We need to accept the blame for our sin before God.

(Bible verse: 1 John 1:9) If we confess our sins, he is faithful and just and will forgive us our sins.

- **A**dmit to God and yourself that you have sinned; that you have left God out of your life and gone your own way.
- **B**elieve that Jesus came to this world to die on the cross to take your punishment so that you can be forgiven.
- **C**ommit your whole life to God. Turn away from living life your way and start living it God's way.

Do this and you will have a healthy relationship with God.

5. Mr & Mrs

Hold a '*Mr & Mrs*' night based on the old TV quiz show, accompanied by a buffet or meal and a short evangelistic talk (Idea 4 gives a suitable outline).

The preparation

You will need to ask two couples beforehand if they will take part, and find out some anecdotes about their engagement, wedding day or married lives. If you have a gregarious, confident character in your church, ask them to be the game show host, and ensure that you have a 'beautiful assistant'.

Set up a seat in one corner of the room with a stereo, headphones and blindfold (in the TV series the contestant sat in a small booth). If you have the resources, why not be creative and decorate the chair, and maybe even erect curtains or a gazebo?

The rules

In the show a small prize was awarded for each correct answer and a star prize if the couple got all of their six questions right. Add extra comedy to the evening by awarding prizes of household goods (e.g. pair of face flannels, rubber gloves, loo brush, etc.) as they did in the recent *Mr & Mrs* re-launch.

One contestant must answer three questions about their partner while their partner wears a blindfold and headphones. The questions are multiple choice and the contestant must choose one of the three answers provided. Once all the questions have been answered, their partner will be invited back and asked to answer the same three questions, with prizes awarded for matching answers. The contestants then swap places and follow the same routine to answer a further three questions. In addition to the small prizes, if all six answers match, the couple win the star prize.

The evening

Start the evening by welcoming the audience and contestants, maybe suggesing that the audience join in with the *Mr & Mrs* theme tune or a familiar song on love and marriage, etc. Introduce the first couple and prompt them to tell the audience their wedding day anecdote, then explain the rules of the game (see above) and ask them to decide who will answer the first three questions.

The questions

Twelve suitable questions are outlined below and for a really professional feel could be typed or written onto question cards.

1. You and your partner decide to have a Saturday night at home with a take away. What pizza topping would <<contestant's name>> prefer?

    Cheese and Tomato; Ham and Pineapple; Meat Feast.

2. The TV programme *Changing Rooms* is sending a team to make over your bedroom. What theme does <<contestant's name>> ask for?

    Modern and trendy; cool and airy; snug and cosy.

3. How would <<contestant's name>> rate their cooking ability?

   Useless, even burns toast; can cook a number of favourites; move over, Delia.

4. You and your partner take a holiday in Greece. What would <<contestant's name>> rather spend time doing?

   Sunbathing; trying out the water sports; exploring ancient sites.

5. Your partner spends a night in alone watching TV. What would <<contestant's name>> watch?

   A soap; a documentary; a quiz show.

6. A questionnaire at work asks your partner to rate their computer ability. What would <<contestant's name>>'s answer be?

   Useless; dabbler; expert.

7. You ask your partner what type of restaurant they would like to visit for a Valentine's meal. What do they say?

   Indian; Chinese; Italian.

8. What would <<contestant's name>> say was their best feature?

   Mouth; eyes; hair.

9. Your partner is going out to the cinema with friends for a birthday treat. What type of film would <<contestant's name>> like to see?

   Romantic comedy; spy thriller; action.

10. Your partner has had a hard day at work. What does
    <<contestant's name>> do to relax?
    Take a bath; listen to music; watch a film.

11. You and your partner have decided to get a dog. What
    type would <<contestant's name>> prefer to have?
    Poodle; German Shepherd; mixed breed rescue dog.

12. You and your partner come back from a winter sports
    holiday. What would your partner tell friends they
    enjoyed most?
    Skiing; snow-boarding; après-ski.

Shrove Tuesday

Introduction

Shrove Tuesday is the day before the Christian season of Lent begins. Across the world it has been a tradition for people to celebrate and have one final fling before the fast! Mardi Gras ('fat Tuesday' in French) is celebrated in New Orleans, carnival ('goodbye to meat' in Latin) in Brazil, and Fasnacht ('fast night') in Germanic Europe. These celebrations are often accompanied by processions, and revellers dress up in masks and costumes, dancing and feasting late into the night. In Britain we celebrate by serving pancakes, traditionally to use up the last of the rich ingredients in the larder (i.e. eggs, milk, butter and sugar). In the market town of Olney in Buckinghamshire they still hold a pancake race, which reputedly started in 1445. In Sedgefield, County Durham, a traditional ball game with no rules has been played in the streets on Shrove Tuesday for 970 years.

Hold a Mardi Gras Ball aimed at youth or adults, or host a Pancake Party aimed at children, youth or families. Both events provide the opportunity to invite guests and to give a short evangelistic address.

6. Mardi Gras Masquerade Ball

A Mardi Gras Ball is a great event to hold, and easy to invite friends to, as it promises to be a fun, exciting and unusual evening in the often uneventful time after Christmas and before Easter. This event could be targeted at youth – join together with other church youth groups to make up numbers if necessary. Alternatively, adults like to let their hair down as well, and the prospect of an evening of Cajun food, dancing and music will encourage church members to invite friends, family and work colleagues along.

The event can be as large or small as you feel you can cope with. If you have a church hall this may be an adequate venue, as long as you are able to create the right atmosphere (e.g. low lighting). Otherwise why not hire a local venue?

Decorate the room in the traditional Mardi Gras colours: purple, green and gold. Use tablecloths, napkins, streamers and helium-filled balloons. Inform people that dress code for the evening is 'carnival', so costumes can be as fantastic as they like; other options include painted faces or masks, or clothes in Mardi Gras colours. Award a prize to the best-costumed male and female, who will be crowned Mardi Gras King and Queen.

Serve Cajun food followed by New Orleans-style coffee (i.e. chicory latte or dark, sweet French roast) and 'king cake', the traditional crown-shaped New Orleans pastry (recipes below). After the meal give a short after-dinner talk. Idea 7 gives the outline for an evangelistic address based on the Mardi Gras colours and their traditional symbolism (purple: justice; gold: power; green: faith).

Hire a jazz band (look under 'Musicians' in the *Yellow Pages*). If your budget won't stretch to hiring a live band, play New Orleans/Mardi Gras/carnival-style CDs. If you are holding a youth ball, you may be advised to have some modern chart music available for later in the evening. For the more adventurous have a limbo stick ready!

7. Talk: 'The Message of Mardi Gras'

Opening illustration

The carnival season of Mardi Gras is celebrated during the weeks between Epiphany (6th January) and Shrove Tuesday, predominantly in the southern states of the USA. 'Mardi Gras' means 'fat Tuesday' in French and is traditionally the final fling before the season of Lent fasting begins. In the mid-eighteenth century, Mardi Gras celebrations were forbidden due to the rowdiness of the festivities. In the early nineteenth century the laws were renounced and Mardi Gras festivities became legal again, with the restriction that masked balls could only be held between 1st January and Shrove Tuesday to stop the population from partying all year round!

In 1872 the Russian Grand Duke Alexis Romanoff came to New Orleans, the capital of Mardi Gras, during carnival time and a group of forty New Orleans businessmen founded a 'krewe' to organize celebrations, including a parade. They adopted Romanoff's three family colours as the official carnival colours in honour of his visit. They said that the colours were symbolic.

Point 1 (sin): Purple – the colour of justice

Do you agree that we live in a world where what is called 'justice' often seems to be injustice? We live in a world where there is much wrong. But we as human beings are the ones who cause the wrong. We do much in our life that God never made us to do.

(Bible verse: Revelation 15:3) Great and marvellous are your deeds, Lord God Almighty. Just and true are your ways, King of the ages.

Point 2 (forgiveness): Gold – the colour of power

Is there anything in your life that you wish you had the power to change? We live in a world where people feel powerless. Their lives are not going the way they would like; their work isn't going the way they would like; the world isn't going the way they would like, and they feel powerless to do anything about it. God is a powerful God who has the power to change things in our lives. We have to allow God to come and change our lives. We are powerless to do anything that can get us to God, so he comes to us.

(Bible verse: Romans 5:6) You see, at just the right time, when we were still powerless, Christ died for the ungodly.

Jesus Christ, God's Son, had the power to forgive wrong, and he still does have that power. He had the love to lay down his own life by dying on the cross. He overcame sin and death by taking the punishment that we deserve for our wrong and then rising again from the dead.

Point 3 (response): Green – the colour of faith

We live in a world where people feel they have nothing worth believing in. But God is totally worth trusting and believing in. Instead of treating us as we deserve, he treats us as we do not deserve. God believes in us, his creation. He felt that we were worth rescuing. That's what Jesus was all about.

(Bible verse: Hebrews 11:6) And without faith it is impossible to please God.

- **A**dmit to God and yourself that you have sinned; that you have left God out of your life and gone your own way.
- **B**elieve that Jesus came to this world to die on the cross to take your punishment so that you can be forgiven.
- **C**ommit your whole life to God. Turn away from living life your way and start living it God's way.

Do this and mean it, and God will forgive you.

8. Pancake Olympics

Hold a Pancake Olympics tournament.

1. Pancake sprint

Each runner must have flipped their pancake three times before reaching the finish line.

2. Pancake relay

At the end of each leg the runner must pass the pancake to their team member by tossing it into their pan from a distance of at least one metre.

3. Pancake flip

Each competitor must flip their pancake as many times as possible in one minute (why not try to break the world record?).

4. Pancake discus

Each competitor must hurl the pancake from a pan as far as possible.

9. Pancake Puzzle

How many words of three letters or more (not counting names) can be made out of the words PANCAKE PARTY?

Work in teams and allow fifteen minutes to complete this word game before collecting the entries and marking them.

Suggested word list

Three letters	Four letters	Five letters	Over five
Ace	Acne	Apace	Apparent
Act	Acre	Apart	Appear
Ant	Area	Arena	Arcane
Any	Arty	Caper	Canary
Ape	Cake	Cater	Carpet
Apt	Cane	Crane	Cranky
Arc	Cape	Crank	Encrypt
Are	Care	Crate	Karate
Ark	Carp	Creak	Nectar
Art	Cart	Crept	Packet
Ate	Cent	Crypt	Panacea
Can	Cyan	Enact	Pantry
Cap	Earn	Entry	Papacy
Car	Kept	Nappy	Papery
Cat	Nape	Paper	Parapet
Cry	Near	Peaky	Parent
Ear	Neat	Peaty	Partake
Eat	Neck	Prank	Prance
Era	Pace	React	Racket
Key	Pack	Recap	Repack
Nap	Pane	Repay	Trance

Three letters	Four letters	Five letters
Nay	Pant	Tacky
Net	Park	Taken
Pan	Part	Taker
Pap	Pate	Taper
Par	Peak	Trace
Pat	Pear	Track
Pay	Peat	Yearn
Pea	Peck	
Pen	Pent	
Per	Pert	
Pet	Pray	
Pry	Prey	
Ran	Pyre	
Rap	Race	
Rat	Rack	
Ray	Racy	
Rye	Rake	
Tan	Rank	
Tap	Rant	
Tar	Rape	
Tea	Rate	
Ten	Reap	
Try	Rent	
Yak	Tack	
Yet	Take	
	Tank	
	Tape	
	Teak	
	Tear	
	Tern	
	Trap	
	Tray	
	Trek	
	Type	
	Yarn	
	Year	

10. Talk: 'Don't Put All Your Eggs in One Pancake'

Opening illustration

Ask members of your audience what their favourite pancake topping is. Ask if any members of the audience have decided to give up anything for Lent.

Point 1 (sin): Giving it up for Lent

Around this time of year many people give things up for a period. Chocolate is one of the most popular. Somehow we recognize the need to give things up. God wants us to give up the things in our lives that are not right.

Imagine I invite you round to my home for pancakes. As I open the box of eggs I notice one of the eggs is off. There are five good ones, but I need six, so I put the bad one in the mixture anyway. I can cover the pancake with all your favourite toppings, but at the end of the day there is enough bad egg in the mixture to spoil the taste and perhaps make you ill.

(Bible verse: James 2:10) For whoever keeps the whole law and yet stumbles at just one point is guilty of breaking all of it.

All of us have broken God's law. The Bible calls this sin, and says that it is what separates us from God.

Point 2 (forgiveness): Bent on living it up

We all want to feel our lives are meaningful. We only get one crack at life, so we make the most of it. God actually wants us to 'live it up', but he also wants us to live it his way. Jesus said in the Bible:

(Bible verse: John 10:10) I have come that they might have life, and have it to the full.

We all try to fill our lives with things because we are missing the vital ingredient: God. Jesus came to deal with the root of our problem: our wrong. We have broken God's law and deserve to be punished. Jesus took that punishment for us on the cross.

Point 3 (response): Give up what's been lent

Our lives are not our own. Every day that we live is in God's plan for us. Each day is given (lent) to us by God. We actually need to give our whole lives up to God, not just a few things at Lent. Jesus gave up his life for you. Will you surrender yours to him?

(Bible verses: 1 Corinthians 6:19–20) You are not your own; you were bought at a price. Therefore honour God with your body.

You can honour God with your body, and it starts by recognizing that God has given you your life and he can take it away from you.

• **A**dmit to God and yourself that you have sinned; that you have left God out of your life and gone your own way.

- **B**elieve that Jesus came to this world to die on the cross to take your punishment so that you can be forgiven.
- **C**ommit your whole life to God. Turn away from living life your way and start living it God's way.

Do this and mean it, and God will forgive you.

11. Shrove Tuesday Traditional Recipes

Pancakes

4 oz (125 g) plain flour
1 egg
½ pint (300 mls) milk
vegetable oil

Recipe makes about 8 pancakes.

1. Beat the egg and milk into half the flour and then gradually add the rest of the flour to make a smooth batter. (Alternatively, mix together for a few seconds using a blender.)
2. Heat the oil in a heavy-based frying pan, run the oil around the pan and pour off any surplus.
3. Pour in just enough batter to coat the bottom of the pan. Cook for 1–2 minutes until golden brown, toss and then cook the other side the same.
4. Pancakes can be kept warm in a low oven, separated by sheets of greaseproof paper.

Serve with traditional lemon and sugar, or alternatively try sliced bananas and whipped cream, strawberries and ice cream, chocolate spread, golden syrup or jam. Pancakes are also delicious with savoury fillings, such as chicken curry, chilli con carne or chicken supreme.

Gumbo

Gumbo is a product of the mix of cultures influencing the New Orleans area: American Indian, French, Spanish and African. It is sold on the streets during the Mardi Gras. The word 'gumbo' is a derivative of the African word '*gombo*', meaning 'okra', and known references to the dish date back to 1805.

3½ lb (1.500 kg) chicken pieces on the bone
1 onion, quartered
celery leaves
1 tsp salt
1 lb (450 g) spicy sausage, sliced ¼″ (5 mm) thick
1 tbsp vegetable oil
2 large onions, chopped
2 green peppers, chopped
2 celery stalks, chopped
3 cloves garlic, crushed
2 cans chopped plum tomatoes
1 lb (450 g) okra, trimmed and sliced
salt and freshly ground black pepper

1. Place chicken, quartered onion, celery leaves and salt into a large heavy saucepan and add at least 2 pints (1.5 litres) of water to cover. Bring to the boil, cover and simmer for 40 minutes. Remove chicken, reserving 2 pints (1 litre) of the stock and discarding onion and celery leaves. Skin, bone and dice chicken. Set stock and chicken aside.
2. Place onions, peppers, celery and garlic in the saucepan and fry in 1 tbsp of oil over a medium heat, stirring constantly until soft.
3. Add chicken, sausage, reserved stock and remaining ingredients. Bring to the boil; reduce heat, and simmer uncovered for 1½ hours.

4. Adjust seasoning if necessary.
5. Serve hot over boiled rice.

New Orleans king cake

This is a traditional iced pastry brought over to New Orleans from France, where king's cakes (or *Gateaux de Rois*) have been made since the seventeenth century. The season of carnival lasts from Epiphany (Twelfth Night) through to Shrove Tuesday (Mardi Gras Day) and it is to commemorate the arrival of the kings at Jesus' stable (traditionally on the twelfth night after Christmas) that the crown-shaped king cake is made during this season. The cake is traditionally decorated with sugar coloured in the Mardi Gras colours of purple, gold and green. Recipe makes enough cake for 20.

1 lb (450 g) flour
4oz (125 g) sugar
1 tsp nutmeg
1 tsp salt
3 oz (85 g) butter
1 tsp lemon zest
½ pt (300 ml) tepid milk and water mixed
1 packet (7 g) fast action dried yeast
5 egg yolks
1 tsp cinnamon
beaten egg, to glaze

Decoration

Green, purple and yellow food colouring (if you can't find purple, use a few drops of red and blue)

9 tbsp granulated sugar
12 oz (350 g) icing sugar

4 tbsp lemon juice
2–5 tbsp water

1. Sieve flour, sugar, nutmeg and salt into a large mixing bowl. Rub in the butter and then stir in the lemon zest.
2. Form a well in the centre of the mixture and add the warm liquid, the dried yeast and the egg yolks. Work together until the mixture is smooth and forms a medium soft dough.
3. Place ball of dough on a lightly floured surface and knead like bread, adding the extra flour if required. (Don't worry if the dough is very sticky. Just keep adding flour slowly and kneading until the dough is no longer sticky.) Knead for about 10 minutes in total, until it is shiny and elastic.
4. Grease a large bowl with butter, and place dough ball in the bowl and rotate until the entire surface is buttered. Cover bowl with a clean tea towel and leave in a warm place for about 1½ hours, or until the dough doubles in size.
5. Remove dough from bowl and place on lightly floured surface. Sprinkle cinnamon over the top and fold the dough ball over, pinching the edges together. Now gently stretch and form the dough into a long roll.
6. Place the roll onto a greased baking sheet and then bend it round to make a ring. Dampen the ends and mould them together.
7. Cover dough with the towel and leave in a warm place for a further 45 minutes until the ring of dough doubles in size.
8. Brush with the beaten egg and bake in middle of a pre-heated oven (5, 190 °C, 375 °F) for 25–35 minutes until golden brown. Cool on a wire rack.

Tip: Use the leftover egg whites to make Mardi Gras meringues. Whisk the egg whites briskly until stiff and retaining peaks; gently whisk in 2 oz (55 g) of sugar per egg white, adding the sugar a little at a time. Divide the mixture into 3 bowls and add food colouring to colour one bowl green, one bowl yellow and one bowl purple. Use a dessert spoon to drop spoonfuls of mixture onto a baking tray lined with greaseproof paper and cook in a very low oven (¼, 100 °C, 225 °F) for 2–3 hours or until dry.

Decoration

1. Place 3 tbsp granulated sugar into a clean, dry jam jar or sealable Tupperware container. Add 4 drops of green food colouring. Seal the jar and shake vigorously for 20 seconds. Empty the coloured sugar onto greaseproof paper and put on one side.
2. Repeat the above for the other 2 colours, ensuring that the jar is clean and dry between colours.
3. Mix together icing sugar, lemon juice and 2 tablespoons of water in a bowl until smooth. If icing is too stiff, add more water until spreadable.
4. Spread icing thickly over top and sides of the cooled cake. Immediately sprinkle the coloured sugars in alternate rows of approximately 2 inch (5 cm) width.

Commonwealth Day/
International Evening

Introduction

Commonwealth Day is an annual event held on the second Monday in March, during which all the fifty-four member countries of the Commonwealth celebrate their links with one another. The Commonwealth currently consists of 1.7 billion people (approximately 30 per cent of the world's population) and has members in Africa, Asia, Europe, the Caribbean, Canada and the South Pacific. Commonwealth Day could be celebrated by a special evening event or by a service on the nearest Sunday. Alternatively, an International Evening could be held at any time throughout the year, either themed on a particular nationality (e.g. an Afro-Caribbean Evening, an Oriental Evening, a Mexican Evening) or encompassing many nationalities together.

12. Talk: 'What Is Jesus For?'

Opening illustration

Someone once said that in a perfect world the cars would all be German, the cooks would all be French, the lovers would all be Italian and it would all be organized by the English. The same person said that in an imperfect world the cars would all be French, the cooks would all be English, the lovers would all be German and it would all be organized by the Italians.

We do live in an imperfect world, but not because of the above. Nevertheless, God loves this imperfect world. One of the most famous verses in the Bible talks about this.

(Bible verse: John 3:16) For God so loved the world that he gave his one and only Son.

God gave his Son Jesus to the world. But why? What is Jesus for?

Point 1 (sin): Jesus is for life, not just for Christmas

You'd never have a baby and leave it in a cot for ever, yet many people do this with Jesus. Jesus was born but he also lived a life. If you leave him in the manger, he will always be a stranger. Jesus has grown up since then! We miss out on the reason for his birth.

Gentle Jesus, meek and mild,
in a manger, the infant child.

But this same Jesus became the one who died on a cross for everyone.

Now that brings us to Easter time.
These are facts, they affect you, they're not just a rhyme.

Jesus' birth was for life!

(Bible verse: Matthew 1:21) And you will give him the name Jesus, because he will save his people from their sins.

Jesus' name gives us an insight into the purpose of his birth and life: to save us from our sins (that is, all the things we do that God doesn't want us to do).

Point 2 (forgiveness): Jesus is for adults, not just for children

Jesus is not a make-believe fairytale character in a story from your childhood. *He isn't make-believe but he does make you believe* when you see him as he really is. Jesus is more interested in your health than your doctor is; he's more interested in your finances than your bank manager is; he's more interested in your family than any relative is; he's more interested in your life than you are. Jesus' life was for death; Jesus' death was for life.

(Bible verse: John 3:16) For God so loved the world that he gave his one and only Son.

For God so loved Nigeria; for God so loved France; for God so loved (fill in your own) that he gave . . . The cross points north and south and east and west. Jesus died for the whole world. He took the punishment for the wrong of the whole world. That includes you.

Point 3 (response): Jesus is for you, not just for me

Jesus is not only for *you* but he's also *for* you. He wants what is best for you. Jesus is not just *my* way to God, he's the *only* way to God. For any culture he's the way to God. He not only crossed the sin divide, he crossed the culture divide.

(Bible verse: John 3:16) For God so loved the world that he gave his one and only Son, that whoever believes in him shall not perish but have eternal life.

It's global but it's personal. God loves the world, and you're in the world. God loves you. Jesus died for you, and you need to respond personally.

- Admit to God that you've not lived your life his way.
- Believe that Jesus died on the cross for you so that you could be forgiven.
- Commit your life to God and his plan for your life.

Do this and mean it, and receive God's forgiveness for yourself.

13. Interview a Christian of a Different Nationality

Interview a Christian who has interesting stories about their life and faith in their country. Maybe a member of your church is of foreign nationality (even people from Northern Ireland, Wales or another part of the country may provide a different view of things). Alternatively, you could contact another church in your area that has a more international congregation and ask if they could send someone to be interviewed. If your event is themed, the interviewee should be of the nationality or group of nationalities being celebrated at the event.

The interview should focus on how the interviewee's culture is different from that of the hosting church (e.g. food, customs, memories of childhood, etc.); what faiths are found in their home country and what church is like there. The interview should culminate by focusing on the interviewee's personal testimony (how they became a Christian, and what it is like living the Christian life in their culture).

Some suggested questions are provided below. The interview should not last more than about fifteen minutes.

* What nationality are you? What is life like in your country?
* What is the prevailing religion in your country and how does this affect people's lives?
* What is church like in your country?
* How did you become a Christian?
* What is it like being a Christian in your country?

14. Decorations, Music and Food from Around the World

Decorate the venue with national flags and items from the nationalities being celebrated. National flag clipart can be found easily on the Internet (try http://dgl.microsoft.com if you use Microsoft Office products) and printed out on A4 paper using a colour printer. You could hold a competition to identify the flags and items if they are unusual. Play music associated with that country as people enter, and maybe teach a song in the native language or perform a traditional dance or song.

Provide some of the national food. International evenings usually attract non-Christian friends because of the good food! The Internet is a good place to find traditional national recipes.

St Patrick's Day/Irish Night

Introduction

St Patrick's Day falls on 17th March each year, but you don't have to be tied down to a date – an Irish Night could be held at any time of the year. The evening could include a quiz, dancing, national food and a short talk (see ideas following).

15. Talk: 'To Be Sure, To Be Sure'

Opening illustration

* Ask how many women are sure of when their husband's birthday is
* Ask how many men are sure of when their wife's birthday is
* Ask how many wives are sure of when their wedding anniversary is
* Ask how many men are sure of when their wedding anniversary is

There are a lot of things that we are not sure of! But there are some things that God wants us to be absolutely sure of.

Point 1 (sin): Be sure you're forgiven

Just imagine if you could be sure that all the wrong things you have ever thought, said or done could be forgiven and not counted against you. Imagine that you spoke to someone to ask for their forgiveness for something you had done against them and they said that they forgave you. Imagine that could happen with every person you have ever wronged.

(Bible verse: Matthew 9:6) But so that you may know that the Son of Man has authority on earth to forgive sins . . .

The whole purpose of Jesus coming to earth was so that we could be forgiven by God. We may not be able to be sure of

75

others' forgiveness, but we can be sure of God's. All the wrong things we have ever thought, said or done can be wiped out once we acknowledge them and ask for God's forgiveness.

Point 2 (forgiveness): Be sure you have everlasting life

Some people request that their body be frozen when they die in the hope that a cure may later be found for what killed them and they can be revived to live for ever. There are lots of things we cannot be sure of, but just imagine you could be sure of living for ever! Just imagine that you could go and live for ever in a place where there is no suffering or pain or tears!

(Bible verse: 1 John 5:13) I write these things to you who believe in the name of the Son of God so that you may know that you have eternal life.

Imagine if you were to die right now and stand before God: could you be sure you would go to heaven? What would you say to God if he asked you why he should let you in?

Point 3 (response): Be sure he lives in you

There are lots of things we cannot be sure of, but just imagine it were possible to be sure that there is a loving, caring God who only has our best interests at heart and is able to take care of us. Wouldn't he be worth getting to know?

(Bible verse: 1 John 4:13) We know that we live in him and he in us, because he has given us of his Spirit.

The Bible teaches us that we can be sure of this God and his presence in our lives. You can be sure of God's forgiveness, a place in heaven when you die and a friendship with God.

Maybe you say, 'I'm not sure if I am ready to know.' You will only be sure when you take a step and say 'Yes' to God.

- **A**dmit to God and yourself that you have sinned; that you have left God out of your life and gone your own way.
- **B**elieve that Jesus came to this world to die on the cross to take your punishment so that you can be forgiven.
- **C**ommit your whole life to God. Turn away from living life your way and start living it God's way.

Do this and mean it, and you will be sure of God's forgiveness.

16. Irish Quiz

The following is an Irish quiz in six rounds. In between each round present an item while the answers are being marked (e.g. ask an Irish person to share their testimony; demonstrate Irish dancing; sing an Irish song). The following questions have been adapted from a number of Irish trivia sites on the Internet.

General knowledge

1. Is a bodhran a drum or a fiddle? (A drum)
2. The Irish beer Murphys is brewed in which Irish town? (Waterford)
3. What is the most common surname in Ireland? (Murphy)
4. What is a currach? (A small boat)
5. Kissing the Blarney Stone is said to confer which talent? (The gift of the gab)

History

1. In which year was Ireland declared a Republic? (1949)
2. What is the oldest heraldic symbol of Ireland? (The harp)
3. What was the Roman name for Ireland? (Hibernia)
4. When was the Battle of the Boyne? (1690)
5. In which century was Ireland converted to Christianity? (Fifth century)

Geography

1. Which city sits upon the River Liffey? (Dublin)
2. Name the four provinces in Ireland. (Leinster, Ulster, Munster, Connaught)
3. What type of rock is the Giant's Causeway made of? (Basalt)
4. Which is the largest county in Ireland? (Cork)
5. Which group of islands in Ireland also give their name to a type of sweater? (The Aran Islands)

Sport

1. Where do the Irish Rugby Union team play at home? (Landsdowne Road)
2. Which Formula One racing team did Eddie Irvine race for in 2002? (Jaguar)
3. Which football club did George Best play for? (Manchester United)
4. Name the only Irish cyclist to have won the Tour de France. (Stephen Roche)
5. Where is the Hogan Stand? (Croke Park)

Affairs of state

1. Who is the Taoiseach of the Republic of Ireland? (Bertie Ahern)
2. What is the currency of the Republic of Ireland? (The Euro)
3. Which three colours make up the Irish flag? (Green, white, orange)
4. What is the Irish House of Representatives called? (Dail Eireann)
5. What is the Celtic language of Ireland? (Irish Gaelic or Erse)

Literature and legend

1. Who, according to popular legend, is supposed to have driven all the snakes from Ireland? (St Patrick)
2. James Joyce's first novel shares its name with which inhabitants of an Irish city? (Dubliners)
3. Who is the female patron saint of Ireland? (St Brigid)
4. Where is the Book of Kells kept? (Trinity College Library, Dublin)
5. Which Irish poet was awarded the Nobel Prize in 1923? (W. B. Yeats)

Entertainment

1. Name the charismatic lead male dancer of the first production of *Riverdance* and then *Lord of the Dance*? (Michael Flatley)
2. Which instrument does Sharon Corr (of the Corrs) play? (Fiddle)
3. In which city was Terry Wogan born? (Limerick)
4. What is Bono from U2's real name? (Paul Hewson)
5. Give the first names of the five members of Westlife. (Bryan, Shane, Mark, Nicky, Kian)

17. Traditional Irish Recipes

Irish stew

Irish stew can be made with mutton, lamb, beef or bacon. However, using slow-cooked mutton provides a delicious flavour. Recipe serves 4.

2 lb (1 kg) boned mutton, diced in 1″ (25 mm) square chunks
2 lb (1 kg) potatoes, peeled and thickly sliced
2 large onions, skinned and thickly sliced
4 medium carrots, peeled and thickly sliced
1 tbsp pearl barley
2 cups (500 ml) water
salt and pepper
chopped fresh parsley

Prepare the ingredients as described.

1. Layer the meat and vegetables in a casserole dish, sprinkling each layer with a little pearl barley and finishing with a layer of potatoes.
2. Season and then pour in the water.
3. Cover with a tight-fitting lid and cook in the oven at gas mark 4, 350°F or 180°C for about 2½ hours. Alternatively, simmer very slowly on the hob in a flame-proof casserole dish or heavy-bottomed saucepan with tight-fitting lid for 3 hours.
4. Garnish with chopped parsley and serve with traditional Irish soda bread.

Barm brack

Barm brack is a traditional Celtic fruit bread made in Ireland, similar to Scottish Selkirk bannock and Welsh bara brith. Serve cold in slices, with butter if desired, like malt loaf with coffee and tea.

8 oz (225 g) plain flour
2 oz (55 g) caster sugar
1 tsp mixed spice
pinch salt
3 tbsp butter
¼ pt (125 ml) lukewarm milk
1 packet (7 g) fast action dried yeast
1 egg, beaten
6 oz (170 g) mixed fruit (currants, sultanas, raisins, candied peel)

1. Sieve the flour, caster sugar, salt and spice into a large mixing bowl and rub in the butter.
2. Form a well in the centre of the mixture and add the warm milk, yeast and egg. Work together until the mixture is smooth and forms a good dough.
3. Place ball of dough on a lightly floured surface and knead like bread for 10 minutes, working the fruit in while kneading.
4. Place dough in a bowl, cover with a clean tea towel and leave in a warm place for about 1 hour, or until the dough doubles in size.
5. Knead lightly and place in a lightly greased 7 inch (18 cm) diameter cake tin, cover and return to the warm place for a further 30 minutes' rising.
6. Bake near the top of a preheated oven at gas mark 6, 400°F or 200°C for 45 minutes.

7. On removing from the oven, glaze with a syrup made from 2 tsp sugar dissolved in 3 tsp boiling water. Cool on a wire rack.

Mother's Day

Introduction

Mothering Sunday is celebrated in Britain on the fourth Sunday in Lent. It is an old tradition and records show that it has been observed since the sixteenth century. Today Mother's Day is a high-profile commercial institution and outside the church the range of cards, presents and flowers marketed every year grows and grows. However, it is likely that the celebration of Mother's Day originated in the Christian festival of 'Refreshment Sunday', when everyone had to revisit the church of their baptism (their 'mother church'), and hence the time became associated with gathering together as families.

Churches of all denominations still celebrate Mothering Sunday and many outside the church still associate the day with a church visit due to their involvement with uniformed groups such as Scouts and Guides. As such it is a good day to hold a special service to provide opportunity for church members to invite their unchurched family members and friends.

18. Talk: 'Some Mothers Do 'Ave 'Em'

Opening illustration

(Before using these, check the *Guinness Book of Records* for updates.)

- The most babies recorded as being born to one woman is sixty-nine.
- The highest number medically recorded at one birth is nine (nonetuplets)
- The most children born to one mother on the same date but in different years is five
- The largest baby born weighed 29 lbs 4 oz
- The longest recorded pregnancy is fifteen months and twenty days

Some mothers do really 'ave 'em!

Point 1 (sin): You've had yours

It is an amazing fact that God knew every one of your babies before you had them and even before they were conceived.

(Bible verses: Psalm 139:13, 15–16) For you created my inmost being; you knit me together in my mother's womb . . . My frame was not hidden from you when I was made in the secret place. When I was woven together in the depths of the earth, your eyes saw my unformed body. All the days ordained for me were written in your book before one of them came to be.

Have you noticed, though, that babies, children and teen-
agers have a bias to rebel? It starts with their first word ('No')
and their first action (to spit the food out) and it goes on
from there.

*(Bible verse: Psalm 51:5) Surely I was sinful at birth, sinful
from the time my mother conceived me.*

The Bible tells us that we were born into sin. Right from the
word go, we have a bias to do wrong and not live life God's
way. Our naughtiness doesn't stop our parents loving us, just
as our sin doesn't stop God loving us. But God does not
accept our behaviour, just as a mum doesn't accept her
child's behaviour.

Point 2 (forgiveness): Mary had hers

Some mothers do 'ave 'em but no woman has ever had a baby
like Mary the mother of Jesus did. How did Mary feel? We
should not forget she was his mum. Sometimes we focus our
attention on Jesus and forget the heartache his mum must
have gone through. I wonder how she felt when one day she
couldn't find him because he had gone off to talk to some
church leaders; when he healed people; when he rode into
Jerusalem on a donkey and everybody was excited and came
out to see him. Do you think she was proud of what her boy
had accomplished? But I also wonder how she felt when they
asked for Barabbas, a murderer, to be freed instead of her son
Jesus who had only done good. And when finally they cru-
cified him, I wonder if everything within her wanted to run up
to the soldiers and start to beat them. Would she have wanted
to shout, 'Get off my boy! He's done nothing wrong'?

*(Bible verse: Matthew 1:21) You are to give him the name
Jesus, because he will save his people from their sins.*

(Bible verse: 1 John 3:5) But you know he appeared so that he might take away our sins. And in him is no sin.

Jesus was born to live, born to die, born to live again. I wonder how Mary felt when she saw her son come back to life.

Point 3 (response): You too can have Jesus

The Saviour of the world was born in Mary so he could be born in you.

(Bible verse: 1 Thessalonians 5:9) For God did not appoint us to suffer wrath but to receive salvation through our Lord Jesus Christ.

You can know God's forgiveness today.

• Admit to God and yourself that you have sinned; that you have left God out of your life and gone your own way.
• Believe that Jesus came to this world to die on the cross and take your punishment so that you could be forgiven.
• Commit your whole life to God. Turn away from living life your way and start living it God's way.

Do this and mean it, and God will forgive you.

19. Short Play: 'The Prodigal Daughter'

A short play for four actors © 2002 by Emma Greenwood, Noel Donaldson and Sarah Hicks.

Cast

MUM:	Mother of Sam and Angie
SAM:	Teenage girl, Angie's younger sister
ANGIE:	Teenage girl, Sam's older sister
OLD LADY:	Elderly woman resting on a park bench

Scene 1

Two sisters are fighting over a pair of jeans when their mum comes in . . .

MUM   Are you two arguing again? What is it this time? Not over those jeans surely!

SAM   It's her fault! She said she didn't like them and I could have them.

ANGIE   That's not true! I didn't say that at all. I said I would think about it. Why does she always have to take what's mine?

MUM   I won't tell either of you again. Stop arguing. Can we have some peace around here?

SAM   Oh, Mum. I'm sorry . . . maybe I should tell you this now . . . it won't be a problem any more. I don't really know how to say this, but I've applied for a job in London.

MUM	London? But where will you live?
SAM	Do you remember Caroline from school? Well, she says I can stay in her flat until I get myself sorted out.
ANGIE	Not Caroline Brown! Since when have you started talking to her?

Mum sits down on the brink of tears and looks at Sam.

MUM	Oh Sam, this doesn't sound like a good idea. What about college?
SAM	I'm sorry, Mum, but I'm gonna pack now and catch the next train. I've had enough. I have to go, and this is my big chance to make something of my life.
MUM	Are you really sure you're doing the right thing?
SAM	Yes, Mum. Look, I've got to pack . . .

Sam makes as if to leave the room, but then stops and turns back.

SAM	Mum . . . is there any chance I can borrow some money? I'll be in touch when I can . . .
MUM	Well, if you're really set on it, I'll transfer your trust fund money from your gran's will into your savings account tomorrow.

Mum breaks down into sobs as Sam walks out.

Scene 2

Sam in a waitress outfit, in the entrance of a London bistro, fighting with Caroline on her mobile phone.

SAM   I can't talk for very long – we're busy tonight
             and the customers on table 6 are a nightmare
             . . . yeah . . . yeah . . . look, Caroline, I just
             need a few more days, then I should have
             enough money to pay the rent . . . Caroline!
             I'm doing two jobs, and I'm trying my best
             . . . no, I haven't bought anything new for
             weeks and you know I haven't been out . . .
             No, the trust money's all gone . . . No, don't
             look for someone else! Please, Caroline, I'll
             get the money.

Sam slumps back against the wall, dejected and tired.

Scene 3

*Sam is sitting on a park bench with her suitcase and bags all
around her. An old lady is sitting on the other end of the
bench.*

OLD LADY   You've got a lot of bags, dear. Are you
             moving home?
SAM   Mmmph.
OLD LADY   *(continues regardless)* When I moved out of
             home when I got married, I only had one box
             of things, and Albert, my husband, bor-
             rowed the works van to come and collect
             them . . . *(sighs)* of course, he's dead now . . .
             poor Albert. Haven't you got anyone to help
             you, love?
SAM   No, not really. I don't need any help. I
             haven't got anywhere to go anyway.
OLD LADY   What about your mum, dearie? A girl can
             always go home to her mum!
SAM   No . . . no . . . I haven't spoken to her in

	months. I don't think she'd have me back anyway.
OLD LADY	Of course she will. Perhaps you should talk to her, love. Ring her – you never know.
SAM	*(slowly and dejectedly)* No . . . no . . . I don't think I can.

Old lady leaves. Sam picks up an old paper that is lying on the pavement and flicks through it before stopping on a page.

SAM	*(reading)* 'Don't forget Mother's Day!' *(gasps)* That's tomorrow! It's Mother's Day tomorrow!

Scene 4

Sam has reached home and is walking past her mum's house on the other side of the road. It is getting dark.

SAM	Things look the same. No, not quite – Angie's got new curtains. My bedroom light's on! *(sighs dejectedly)* Mum always threatened to take in lodgers when we moved out for college. Is someone else in my room now? Oh, I can't face them. I'll just put the card through the door and then go.

Sam creeps up to the door and pushes the card through the letterbox and then walks slowly back down the path. Mum picks up the card, opens it and then opens the door and calls after Sam.

MUM	Sam!
SAM	Mum . . .
MUM	Sam, have you come home?

SAM   Oh Mum . . . I can't . . . I'm so sorry . . . I've
                spent all the money and . . .
MUM   But this is where you belong. I've kept your
                room the way you like it, hoping you'd come
                back.
SAM   But Mum, I never rang.
MUM   Sam, I'm just glad you're home.

Embrace.

20. A Gift for Mum

Get the children in Sunday school to make marzipan daffo-
dils for their mothers. Use yellow marzipan and colour half
of it green with food colouring. You will need round and
star-shaped biscuit cutters.

1. Use biscuit cutters to cut one large circle from the green
   marzipan and one small circle plus a star from the
   yellow marzipan.

2. Attach the star to the green marzipan.

3. Pinch together the centre of the small yellow circle to make a rosette.

4. Attach the rosette to the centre of the star. Make six imprints in the centre of the flower to represent stamens.

Easter

Introduction

Easter used to be a time when many people thought of attending church, but this is no longer the case. Due to aggressive marketing of Easter consumables, Easter has become more about chocolate eggs, bunnies and chicks, and less about Jesus Christ. Schools no longer teach the Christian Easter message as a matter of course, and the popular media pay little attention to any relevance that church might have at this time. Hence, if we expect the unchurched to attend services at Easter we must launch an awareness campaign. People need to be reminded of the relevance of Easter and the existence of special Easter services before they choose to accept or reject them. Before you plan an Easter strategy, you should realize that raising the profile of your church's Easter services may take a number of years. You should adopt a long-term strategy and manage the expectations of church members. Don't be disappointed if few people attend the first year that the campaign is launched.

When planning events and services to hold over the Easter period, consider those you are trying to reach. Recognize that although many people would like to celebrate special times of the year in a family/community atmosphere, this is not always possible. In today's fractured society, many families are widely dispersed and some people have lost those closest to them. Think specifically about the elderly, those with young families and those alone over the Easter period. Many churches hold children's Easter clubs and Family Services, but think also of holding a bank holiday picnic or fun day, performing a passion play, visiting residential homes and hospitals or putting on a special Easter lunch for the elderly and alone.

Advertise your events and services widely in an appealing and friendly manner: in local shops, local press and the local community. Hold some open air events and encourage church members to invite friends and family.

21. Talk: 'Happy Easter'

Opening illustration

- Ask members of the congregation what their favourite egg is.
- Ask members of the congregation what is the most eggs they have ever received.
- Ask members of the congregation what is the quickest they have eaten their eggs.

At Easter we think a lot about eggs, but what is Easter about? Let's crack it open.

Point 1 (sin): Eggs with surprises

We love to give and receive eggs at Easter, but this is by no means a recent custom. Easter eggs were given as gifts by the ancient Greeks, Persians and Chinese at their spring festivals. Even as early as the Middle Ages, coloured eggs were given as gifts at Easter. The accounts of King Edward I for the year 1290 include the expense of purchasing hundreds of eggs to be distributed to his household.

A pope even prayed over an egg in 1700, thanking God for its meaning. The egg was a symbol to early Christians of Jesus' resurrection and new life. They were forbidden during Lent but reintroduced on Easter Sunday, both as part of the feasting and as gifts for family, friends and servants. So, instead of leaving Jesus' resurrection to the end, let's start with it.

Easter is not about 'Kinder surprises' – it's about a 'King who rises'. Jesus said:

(Bible verse: John 14:19) Because I live, you also will live.

The very fact that Jesus came back to life means that you and I can have new life, a fresh start. Jesus promises new life to all who believe in him. Jesus had a sign nailed to his cross labelling him 'King of the Jews'. This King of the Jews did rise again after his death. Jesus is not only the King of the Jews, he is the King of the whole world, who died and rose again.

Point 2 (forgiveness and response): Hot cross buns

Hot cross buns! Hot cross buns!
One a penny,
Two a penny,
Hot cross buns!
If you have no daughters,
Pray, give them to your sons!
One a penny,
Two a penny,
Hot cross buns!

Easter breads throughout Europe are very similar. All are yeast based, sweet and enriched with eggs and dried fruit. In Russia, Greece and Italy they are single large loaves or cakes, while others like ours are made into little individual buns. The traditional hot cross bun recipe is flour, milk, sugar, butter, eggs, currants and spices such as cinnamon and nutmeg. Normally we have a pastry with a cross baked on the top, but it can also be cut into the bun. In America the cross is often fashioned out of icing. In Scotland the hot cross bun is usually more highly spiced than the English variety.

The origins of the hot cross bun are not certain. Some speak of an English widow whose son went off to sea and she promised to bake a bun for him every Good Friday. When he did not return she continued to bake a hot cross bun for him each year and hung it in the bakery window, confident that one day he would return. The English people kept the tradition for her even after she passed away.

However nice hot cross buns are, fresh from the oven with lashings of creamy butter, Easter is *not* about a 'cross on a bun' but about a 'Son on a cross'.

(Bible verse: Galatians 2:20) The Son of God, who loved me and gave himself for me.

The whole thrust of Easter is that Jesus Christ lived a life that made a difference and died a death that made an even bigger difference. He then came back from the dead to prove he was who he said he was. Jesus came to take the punishment for our wrong. By accepting what Jesus did for us on the cross we can come alive spiritually and know God himself.

- Admit to God and yourself that you have sinned; that you have left God out of your life and gone your own way.
- Believe that Jesus came to this world to die on the cross to take your punishment so that you could be forgiven.
- Commit your whole life to God. Turn away from living life your way and start living it God's way.

Do this and mean it, and God will forgive you.

22. Puppet Show: 'Hot Cross Herbie'

Puppet shows are always popular with children, and it is often easier to get volunteers because even shy people who would not feel comfortable acting can work a puppet. Puppet shows are best performed to prerecorded soundtracks: these can be produced by your puppet team or purchased from specialist puppet ministry groups.

For puppet resources, including scripts and soundtracks, contact:

The Chrestos Trust
PO Box 315
Winchester
Hants SO22 4BB

One Way UK
Unit D1 Acre Business Park
Acre Road
Reading
Berkshire RG2 0SA
www.onewayuk.com

Hot Cross Herbie

A puppet play for six puppets © 2001 by Neil Simpson of the Chrestos Trust and David Simpkin.

Cast

HERBIE:	Not very bright
JAZZ:	Herbie's clever friend
PETER:	One of Jesus' disciples, speaks with northern accent
SERVANT:	Girl working in the High Priest's house in Jerusalem
PILATE:	Roman governor
MARY:	Jesus' mother

Scene 1

Enter Herbie, singing.

HERBIE   We wish you a merry Easter, we wish you a merry Easter, we wish you a merry Easter and a happy new . . .

Enter Jazz.

JAZZ   What are you doing?

HERBIE   I'm singing Easter carols.

JAZZ   Easter carols?

HERBIE   Yeah, Easter carols.

JAZZ   Easter carols?

HERBIE   Yeah, we're all going to sit round the Easter tree and . . . and eat Easter cake and Father Easter is going to come and . . . and . . . have I said something wrong?

JAZZ   Easter carols? Easter trees? Easter cake? Father Easter? You idiot, it's not *Easter* carols, it's *Christmas*!

HERBIE   Is it? What, already? Oh doesn't time fly? *(Other puppets pop up wearing party hats and singing)*

We wish you a merry Christmas, we wish you a merry Christmas, we wish you a . . .

JAZZ   No! *(Other puppets down)* I don't mean it's Christmas now, I mean it's . . . Look. It's not Christmas, it's Easter! Now what's all this Easter carols and Easter trees thing?

HERBIE   Well . . . I don't actually know anything about Easter, so I thought I'd . . . sort of . . . rerun Christmas.

JAZZ   Rerun Christmas? You can't just rerun Christmas.

HERBIE   Why not? They do on TV.

JAZZ   Well, for a start I've only just finished eating turkey sandwiches from last Christmas. Look, if you really don't know anything about Easter, I'll tell you about Easter. In fact, step inside my puppet stage and I'll take you there, back to the first Easter.

HERBIE   What d'you mean, you'll take me there?

JAZZ   Puppet stages can travel back in time. Didn't you know?

HERBIE   No!

JAZZ   You see, I finished making this one in 2025.

HERBIE   Oh!

Exit Herbie and Jazz. Time travelling music.

Scene 2

Garden of Gethsemane. Enter Herbie and Jazz.

HERBIE   Cor! That was amazing! You know, that puppet stage is much bigger on the inside than it looks on the outside! Odd that! So where are we now?

JAZZ   Gethsemane.

HERBIE   Bless you!

JAZZ	*This* is the Garden of Gethsemane. Near Jerusalem.
HERBIE	*(looks out at audience)* Are you sure?
JAZZ	*(patiently)* Yes. Look, here comes Peter.
HERBIE	Oh right . . . Peter. Err . . . who's Peter?
JAZZ	You know! He's one of the disciples.
HERBIE	A di-cycle. *(pause)* Is that like a bi-cycle? How many wheels does he have?
JAZZ	What? No! Not di-cycle, a di-sci-ple. One of Jesus' followers.
HERBIE	Well, he's not following anybody at the moment – look at the speed he's going. If you ask me, it's the other way round. I think there are people following him!

Peter enters.

PETER	Are they still after me?
HERBIE	See! I told you. Are who still after you?
PETER	The temple guards. They've just arrested Jesus. It was that traitor Judas's fault. Led them right to us, he did. One of Jesus' own disciples!
HERBIE	You what?
JAZZ	I think you'd better start from the beginning.
PETER	Are you sure?
JAZZ	You'd better.
PETER	Right from the beginning?
JAZZ	Right from the beginning.
PETER	OK. God made the world. And on the first day God created the heavens and the earth . . .
JAZZ	Maybe that's too far back. What about the beginning of *this* story.
PETER	Oh right! Well, about three years ago my brother Andrew came and told me that he had met the Messiah.

HERBIE   The what?

PETER   The Messiah; *(realizing Herbie doesn't understand)* the Christ, *(realizing Herbie still doesn't understand)* God's chosen one. *(realizing Herbie STILL doesn't understand)* Look. We Jews have been expecting God's special person to come for ages, to put everything right in the world. That person is called the Messiah. Of course not everybody believes Jesus is the Messiah, and he's upset a lot of the religious leaders. They don't believe he's the Messiah. They just want to get rid of him.

HERBIE   Why are they trying to get rid of him?

JAZZ   Well, if he is the Messiah then they need to do what he says, and they don't want to do that.

HERBIE   Why not? I mean, if he's God's chosen one why wouldn't they want to do what he says?

JAZZ   Well, sometimes we know what we *ought* to do, but we still do what we *want* to do. It's like that.

PETER   Yes, and now they've arrested Jesus. Look, I've got to get going.

Peter exits.

HERBIE   No, wait!

Herbie and Jazz exit. Chase music. Herbie chases Peter.

Scene 3

Herbie enters.

HERBIE   Oh, I lost him! I think he went into this building. I've been waiting around for ages to see if he comes out.

Servant enters.

SERVANT   Hello, I'm not meant to be here.

HERBIE   That's a funny name.

SERVANT   No, I mean I shouldn't really be here. I should
          be getting on with my jobs. You see, I work for
          the High Priest. Now when I say High Priest, I
          don't mean he's tall – actually he's quite short
          really. He's not the tall priest, he's the High
          Priest. I mean he's the big priest. No! I don't
          mean he's fat, I mean he's . . . Look! There are
          lots of priests, but the High Priest is the most
          important one of the lot. He's the boss priest.

HERBIE   Err . . . yeah? OK. Umm . . . I'm looking for
          Peter. Have you seen him?

SERVANT   Who?

HERBIE   Peter. He's about my height, head full of foam.
          You can't miss him.

SERVANT   Hang on! Did he have a northern accent?

HERBIE   Yes, that's him!

SERVANT   Yes, there was someone like that. The soldiers
          had brought Jesus to see the High Priest and all
          the religious leaders at the High Council. Now,
          when I say High Council, I don't mean tall . . .

HERBIE   Yes, yes . . . we've done all that.

SERVANT   So, anyway, they brought Jesus to the High
          Council to hear his case, but they couldn't get
          anyone to agree about what he was supposed to
          have done wrong, so they sent him to Pilate.

HERBIE   They sent him to the pilot? What, on an aero-
          plane?

SERVANT   Don't be silly. We haven't invented aeroplanes
          yet. Pilate is the name of the Roman Governor.
          But . . . I did see your friend Peter.

HERBIE   Did he try and rescue Jesus?

SERVANT   No. He just sat by the fire.

HERBIE   What?

SERVANT   Well, I was just crossing the courtyard to talk to the high servant.

HERBIE   Yeah, yeah, we know . . . the boss servant.

SERVANT   No. He's just very tall.

HERBIE   (*crestfallen*) Oh!

SERVANT   Anyway, I was crossing the courtyard and there was Peter, sitting by the fire. So I went up to him and said, ''Ere! Are you with that Jesus?' And he said, 'No, I don't know what you're talking about!' and walked off. Well, a bit later I was talking to one of the other servants and he saw your friend Peter over by the gate and told everyone, 'This man was with Jesus of Nazareth.' And then Peter said he wasn't. Well, he would, wouldn't he? And then some other people came over and said, 'You *must* be with Jesus! You've even got the same accent as him.' And your friend Peter told them, 'God's honour, I don't even know the man!' And then . . . a cockerel crowed and Peter went all white and ran away. Talking of which, I'd better get back to work. I can't stand here talking all day.

HERBIE   Why not?

SERVANT   I haven't got any more lines.

Exit Servant. Enter Peter, distraught.

PETER   I've really messed it up now. I've done exactly what Jesus said I would.

HERBIE   Well, that's good, isn't it?

PETER   No! He said I'd mess it up and I have! Three times I said I didn't know him. That's exactly

what Jesus said would happen before the cockerel crowed. I'd better get out of here.

Exit Peter.

HERBIE   No! Wait! . . . Oh.

Exit Herbie. Herbie chases Peter.

Scene 4

Enter Jazz.

JAZZ   I've lost both of them. Herbie and Peter!

Enter Pilate.

PILATE   You! What are you doing here?
JAZZ   I'm talking to the audience.
PILATE   Who?
JAZZ   Them.
PILATE   Oh, the Great Unwashed . . . Well, what are you
         doing in my house?
JAZZ   Your house? Who are you?
PILATE   I am Pontius Pilate, Roman Governor of Judea.
JAZZ   Oh, you're the man they took Jesus to see. We're
         trying to tell the story of Easter and we need
         you to tell your side of the story.
PILATE   Well, of course you would – I'm so important.
         That's why they brought Jesus to me in the first
         place. They wanted to kill him and they could-
         n't without my permission, so they dragged him
         over to me.
JAZZ   And you found him guilty?
PILATE   Err . . . No.

JAZZ   So you let him go?

PILATE   Err . . . No. I sent him to King Herod.

JAZZ   Oh! King Herod found him guilty?

PILATE   Err . . . No. King Herod sent him back to me.

JAZZ   And *then* you found him guilty?

PILATE   Err . . . No.

JAZZ   So you let him go?

PILATE   Err . . . No. I offered to, but all the priests said they wanted Jesus killed and I was too frightened to stand up to them. Anyway, they said they would tell the Emperor that I was allowing dangerous men to walk free.

JAZZ   And were you?

PILATE   Yes – the priests who were causing the riots!

JAZZ   So what did you do to Jesus?

PILATE   Well, I knew he was innocent, so I had him flogged and beaten and sentenced to be killed on a cross.

JAZZ   Was that fair?

PILATE   Sorry?

JAZZ   I mean, was it right?

PILATE   Err . . . Sorry? You've lost me there.

JAZZ   I mean, was it the right thing to do – to kill an innocent man?

PILATE   Look, if I hadn't killed him, the priests would have told the Emperor that I wasn't doing my job properly and he might have had me killed. I decided that I was far more important than Jesus. It was him or me.

JAZZ   So you let an innocent man die in your place?

PILATE   I suppose so. Look, I can't stop here all day talking to you – I've got much more important things to do.

JAZZ   Oh, one last thing. I'm looking for my friend Herbie. Have you seen him?

PILATE	No. If I find him, do you want me to kill him?
JAZZ	No!
PILATE	Beat him up?
JAZZ	No!
PILATE	Have him flogged?
JAZZ	No! I want you to help him.
PILATE	Help him? I'm not very good at that. I'll see what I can do.

Exit Pilate.

| JAZZ | Oh, there's Herbie now! Herbie! Come back! Oh! |

Exit Jazz. Jazz chases Herbie.

Scene 5

Enter Herbie.

| HERBIE | Every time I think I've caught up with Peter he slips away. I'll ask this lady if she's seen him. Excuse me! |

Enter Mary.

MARY	Oh sorry! I was miles away.
HERBIE	No you weren't, you were right here.
MARY	No, I meant my thoughts were miles away.
HERBIE	Oh yeah, I have that problem sometimes. My thoughts are miles away and my brain is completely empty.
MARY	No, what I meant was, I was thinking about something else.
HERBIE	Oh.

MARY   Yes, you see I'm Mary, and I was thinking about
            my son Jesus. He's just been killed on a cross.

HERBIE   Oh no!

MARY   Yes, they've killed him and I don't understand
            it. The angel said he was the Messiah.

HERBIE   Excuse me? What angel?

MARY   The angel who spoke to me before Jesus was
            born. He told me Jesus was the Messiah, God's
            chosen one, who was going to put everything
            right between God and man. But now they've
            gone and killed him. That can't be right, can it?

Mary runs off crying.

HERBIE   No wait, come back! Oh, she's gone.

Enter Jazz.

JAZZ   Oh, there you are. I've been looking for you
            everywhere.

HERBIE   I've just met Mary, Jesus' mum. She says that
            Jesus has been killed on a cross. That can't be
            right, can it? I mean, if Jesus is the Messiah, he
            wouldn't have to let himself be killed, would
            he?

JAZZ   He wouldn't have to, but he might allow
            himself to if it helps other people. Look, why
            don't we get back in the puppet stage and nip
            forward a couple of days and see what happens
            next?

HERBIE   Hey! This is like pushing the fast forward
            button. Wow!

Exit Herbie and Jazz. Time travelling music.

Scene 6

Enter Herbie and Jazz.

HERBIE	You know, that puppet stage *is* bigger on the inside! Funny that! Where are we?
JAZZ	Jerusalem.
HERBIE	Bless you. You'd better watch that doesn't turn into a cold.
JAZZ	No! We are *in* Jerusalem. It's a couple of days after Jesus was killed.
HERBIE	You mean the audience have been sitting there all that time?
JAZZ	Well, they've probably got their own time machines.
HERBIE	Oh yeah, clever! So why are we here?
JAZZ	We're going to find out what Jesus did afterwards.
HERBIE	After what?
JAZZ	After he died.
HERBIE	*(pause)* Hang on! I'm the stupid one around here. What do you mean 'what Jesus did after he died'? He didn't do anything. You don't do anything after you die, do you? You don't die and then think, 'Hang on, did I put the milk bottles out? I'd better go back and check!' *(sarcastic)* What did Jesus do after he died?
JAZZ	Look, there's Mary. We'll ask her.

Enter Mary.

MARY	He's alive! He is alive!
HERBIE	Who is?
MARY	Jesus! He's alive!
HERBIE	I thought he was dead.

MARY   He was!

HERBIE   But you're saying he's alive.

MARY   Yes! He was dead, but now he's alive. The door of the tomb has been opened and he's not there any more.

HERBIE   Were there any milk bottles outside?

MARY   *(puzzled)* What?

JAZZ   Don't worry about him. I think with all this time travel his brain hasn't caught up.

MARY   Well, some of the women who knew him went to the tomb and they were expecting to find the stone in the way blocking the entrance, but instead the tomb was open and they met two men . . . well, they *looked* like men. And these two men told them that God had raised Jesus from the dead and that he is alive! I'm just off to tell the others.

HERBIE   She's happy. *(pause)* But I still don't understand. Why did God send the Messiah? Why did he allow him to die on a cross? Why has he been raised from the dead?

JAZZ   I think we need to pop forward a few weeks. Come on.

HERBIE   You know, it's lucky the scriptwriter had this time machine; he would have found it much harder to tell the story without it!

Exit Herbie and Jazz.

Scene 7

Enter Herbie and Jazz.

HERBIE   Now tell me again. Where are we?

JAZZ   Jerusalem. Only this time a few weeks after Jesus rose from the dead.

HERBIE   Oh . . . why?

JAZZ   To meet Peter. Look, there he is!

Enter Peter.

PETER   Hello! What are you doing here?

JAZZ   Last time I saw you, you were really scared, because the temple guards were after you.

HERBIE   Last time I saw you, you were really sad, because you'd let Jesus down.

PETER   Yeah, well, that was before Jesus rose from the dead. You see, after Jesus rose from the dead he came and found me and he forgave me for messing it up. Even though I lied and said I didn't know him, he forgave me. I think it's great!

HERBIE   Oh, that *is* great, but I still don't understand what all this Easter bit is about.

PETER   Easter is all about Jesus dying on a cross and being buried and being raised from the dead.

HERBIE   Yeah, yeah, I know all that, but *why*? Why be killed? Why be buried? Why be raised from the dead? I now know what happened at Easter, but *why*?

PETER   Oh . . . why! Well, you know I told you that Jesus forgave me?

HERBIE   Yeah.

PETER   That meant he didn't count all the wrong things I'd done against me – it's as if I've never hurt him.

HERBIE   Yeah?

PETER   Well, when Jesus died on that cross he was taking the punishment for all the wrong things we've done, and he was forgiving us, so it's as if we've never hurt God.

HERBIE   Oh! Hey, that's good!

PETER   Yeah, that's why I'm so happy, and God's given me the courage and the love to tell others, so I'm off to do that. Bye!

Exit Peter.

HERBIE   Yeah. Bye! 'Ere – I think I know enough about Easter now to organize something about it.

JAZZ   Too late.

HERBIE   Too late?

JAZZ   Yes, we've run out of time.

HERBIE   So all these people won't hear the story of Easter?

JAZZ   Well, I've got a feeling they might have heard it.

HERBIE   Really? Who told them?

Exit Herbie and Jazz.

HERBIE   *(Offstage)* 'Ere, you don't think we could go back twenty minutes in your time machine and tell them the story, do you? . . . Why not? . . . What do you mean I've already told them the story?

23. Art and Craft Gallery

Many churches hold an Easter holiday kids' club, but if your resources will not stretch to a week's programme, why not invite children to spend a morning or afternoon producing Easter related art and craft? Then host an Easter Art Gallery in the church on Easter Sunday and invite parents to come to the Easter Sunday service and stay for refreshments and a look at the gallery afterwards.

Some suggestions for creating Easter pictures include:

* Mosaics: use 'tiles' cut out of colour magazines
* Collages: with pasta, beads, wool, cotton wool, cloth, etc.
* Sprays: using spray bottles and straws
* Etchings: colour a piece of card with bright wax crayons, then colour over with black crayon and etch out a picture using a pointed object
* Rubbings: create a picture and then colour it in with wax crayon, rubbing over different textures (e.g. pavement, bark, embossed wallpaper) in different areas of the picture (e.g. character's clothing)
* Washes: draw the picture in white wax (use a white candle) and then wash over it with water-based poster paint

The pictures should be based on the Easter theme. It may be an idea to tell the Easter story to the children before they start their pictures, as it may be unfamiliar to some (you could perform the puppet show in Idea 22). Aim to produce large pictures, as these will look better displayed in the gallery. Take time to think about how the pictures will look best in the gallery: will you mount them or frame them with card frames? Make sure you know which child produced which artwork so that you can make name cards to put with the pictures.

Father's Day

Introduction

Sonora Dodd came up with the idea of Father's Day in 1908 while attending a Mother's Day service in Washington State, USA. Her father had selflessly reared her and her five siblings after the death of their mother, and she felt that he and other fathers deserved to be celebrated in the way that mothers had been for centuries. Father's Day falls on the third Sunday in June.

Although not a celebration with traditional Christian origins like Mothering Sunday, the analogies that can be drawn from the theme are obvious. God is the Father of Jesus. He is also our Father and we are his children. Hence it is not an unnatural link to talk about God the Father at a Father's Day event.

24. Talk: 'God's Conveyor Belt'

Opening illustration

We've all seen the TV programme *The Generation Game*, where the final contestants sit in front of two sliding doors, and passing before them on the conveyor belt are various prizes. Of course, there is always a cuddly toy. The idea of the conveyor belt is that you win the items you remember. If God had a conveyor belt, what would be on it? Well, there would be many things, so let's just mention a few of God's amazing gifts here.

Point 1 (sin): On God's conveyor belt – freedom

Well worth having. If you were in prison, the greatest gift you could ever receive would be freedom.

(Bible verse: John 8:36) So if the Son sets you free, you will be free indeed.

The truth is, we are all in a prison. We aren't free to be the people God wants us to be. It's hard to break bad habits: we have lived lives that habitually leave God out. The Bible calls this sin, and it is from this that we need setting free. God is offering you freedom – do not let it pass by.

Point 2 (forgiveness): On God's conveyor belt – forgiveness

Again, well worth having. I don't know if you have ever heard someone say to you, 'I forgive you.' Wonderful stories are told of people who have not spoken for years and they finally get round to forgiving each other. It is wonderful when forgiveness takes place.

(Bible verse: 1 John 4:14) And we have seen and testify that the Father has sent his Son to be the Saviour of the world.

God was the greatest Father with the greatest Son. They were the greatest Father and Son team. God sent his own Son to this world as an 'I forgive you' statement. God wants to forgive *you*. He sent Jesus to take the punishment for your wrong so that you could have contact with him. God is offering you forgiveness – do not let it pass by.

Point 3 (response): On God's conveyor belt – your future

Many people would love to know what their future holds. They would love to be able to make the right decisions. God isn't saying that he will show you what your future is, but he will lead you in what is best for your future.

(Bible verse: Jeremiah 29:11) 'For I know the plans I have for you,' declares the Lord, 'plans to prosper you and not to harm you, plans to give you hope and a future.'

God is a loving Father and longs to have a relationship with you. He knows what is best for you. Because Jesus died, we can be forgiven for not following God's plan and can be empowered to live out God's plan as he shows it to us. God is offering you a good future – do not let it pass by.

- Admit to God and yourself that you have sinned; that you have left God out of your life and gone your own way.

- **B**elieve that Jesus came to this world to die on the cross to take your punishment so that you could be forgiven.
- **C**ommit your whole life to God. Turn away from living life your way and start living it God's way.

Do this and mean it, and God will set you free, forgive you and lead you in your future.

25. The Generation Game

Hold a *Generation Game* night, based on the TV game show, accompanied by a buffet or meal and a short evangelistic talk (Idea 24 gives a suitable outline).

The preparation

You will need to arrange four teams of father plus daughter or son beforehand and find out some anecdotes about them (most embarrassing moment, bravest thing they've ever done, etc.). If you have a gregarious, confident character in your church, ask them to be the game show host and ensure that they have a 'beautiful assistant'. Three ideas for games are outlined below.

The rules

Two teams compete in Game One, the other two teams compete in Game Two. The winners of both rounds take part in the final.

The games

Game One: CREATIVE CAPERS

Description: 'A chance to show us how good you are with your hands. Our professional will demonstrate their special creative skill before you get the chance to try it out for your-selves!'

124

Ask one of your church members to demonstrate a creative skill that they have (e.g. flower arranging, cake decorating, caricature artist, etc.). The demonstration should be carefully planned beforehand so that it takes no longer than three minutes.

Introduce the 'professional' to the audience with a little bit of 'banter' (how long have they been practising their skill? etc.). During the demonstration the professional or the game show host should keep up a running commentary to hold the audience's interest. Ensure that the professional and their work can be clearly seen by the audience and both sets of contestants.

When the contestants take their turn, again ensure that their attempts can be clearly seen as they take shape. The contestants should all make their attempts at the same time, side by side. Once the allotted three minutes is up, invite the professional back to mark the attempts. Scores should be given out of ten and should not be too harsh. The professional should explain the reasons for the marks, looking for positive as well as negative points.

Game Two: TONGUE TWISTING

Description: 'In this game you will be given tongue twisters to recite as fast as you can. Points will be awarded for accuracy and speed!'

Each tongue twister should be written on a flip chart sheet so that both the contestants and the audience can see. Allow the audience to have a quick attempt after the contestants have attempted each one.

Round one: How many times can each of the following tongue twisters be said correctly in five seconds? Award a point per correct recitation. The judge must listen very carefully!

- Flash message!
- Four furious friends fought for the phone
- Stupid superstition
- World Wide Web
- Eleven benevolent elephants
- Willie's real rear wheel

Round two: Who can recite each of the following tongue twisters fastest and most accurately? Each person is allowed three attempts at each twister. The judge awards five points to the best contestant each time.

- If Stu chews shoes, should Stu choose the shoes he chews?
- How much ground would a groundhog hog, if a groundhog could hog ground? A groundhog would hog all the ground he could hog, if a groundhog could hog ground
- Black background, brown background
- Seven slick slimey snakes slowly sliding southward

The Final: ACTING UP

Description: 'In this game you will get your chance to star in a pantomime!'

Ask your church drama group, or some confident members of your church, to rehearse the following short scene from the pantomime 'Aladdin'. Use colourful costumes and props, and if you have the resources paint a backdrop.

After the professionals have acted the scene, the actors are introduced to the audience. Anakadin and Widow Twanky then drop out and are replaced by one set of contestants, who are taken off to quickly change while the other set of contestants are taken into a back room so they do not gain an unfair advantage from seeing the scene again.

In turn each set of contestants joins the cast to act out Scene 3 of the pantomime. If required, the professionals should help them to get into place during the scene and by prompting lines.

After both sets of contestants have acted out the scene, one of the professionals is asked to award points out of ten, explaining the reason for the marks and making positive comments as well as giving humorous constructive criticism.

Aladdin

Cast

NARRATOR/ANAKADIN'S ASSISTANT
ALADDIN
WIDOW TWANKY
PRINCESS
ANAKADIN
GENIE OF THE RING

The action takes place outside Aladdin's palace.

Scene 1

NARRATOR   Aladdin was left to live in poverty with his mother when his father died unexpectedly at an early age. However, after double-crossing a wicked magician, Aladdin becomes the master of the Genie of the Lamp, wishes for riches and marries the king's daughter. After a week or so of married bliss . . .

Enter Princess, Aladdin and Widow Twanky, Twanky with an exaggerated limp on one foot.

ALADDIN   *(addressing the Princess)* . . . and so, I'm taking my mother to town to buy her some

	new shoes – she has another bunion this morning. Goodbye, my sweet Princess . . . I shall return! Come on, Mummy, we'll soon have your poor little tootsies all comfy.
TWANKY	Oh Aladdin, my son, my son! You are so good to me! Do you know, I think I saw just the pair this morning . . .
ALADDIN	Come on, Mother, or else the shops will be shut for lunch.

Aladdin and Widow Twanky exit.

| PRINCESS | Aladdin's such a kind man and so good to his mother! I can't believe I've met such a wonderful man, and so wealthy as well! |

Scene 2

Enter Anakadin and his Assistant, disguised as a poor trades-man and his son.

ANAKADIN	New for old! New for old! New lamps for old!
ASSISTANT	Good lady, I can see you have sense! My father here will exchange new lamps for old. Just present us with any of your dirty, smelly, sooty, mucky, nasty, grimy, grotty, gross old lamps and we will give you a brand new one; a shiny, sparkling, shimmering, gleaming, brilliant, burnished, lovely, lustrous new lamp!
PRINCESS	Well, when you put it like that . . .
ASSISTANT	*(interrupts)* A shiny, sparkling, shimmering, gleaming, brilliant, burnished, lovely, lus-trous . . .
PRINCESS	*(interrupts)* Yes, yes! Done – it's a deal! *(to*

the audience) You see, on his bedside table Aladdin keeps a nasty dirty . . .

ASSISTANT   *(interrupts)* smelly, sooty, mucky, grimy, grotty, gross . . .

PRINCESS   *(interrupts)* . . . nasty, dirty old lamp that I've been meaning to clean for some time now. And now I don't have to! I can just exchange it for a . . . *(pauses and looks at the Assistant warily)* for a new one *(says 'new one' and swaps lamps very quickly before the Assistant gets the chance to start his list of adjectives again).*

The Assistant passes the old lamp to Anakadin, who throws off his disguise and laughs long and evilly, striding around the stage and showing off the lamp to the audience. The Princess looks startled and alarmed.

ANAKADIN   I am no meagre tradesman, no lamp seller! No! I am Anakadin! The great magician! Double-crossed by your snivelling worm of a husband Aladdin. But now I am Master of the Lamp and the genie will submit to me!

Strides off with a loud, evil laugh. Princess starts to wail and runs off opposite side of stage.

Scene 3

Enter Aladdin and Widow Twanky with shoe boxes piled high in their arms. Short slapstick routine follows (preferably to music), involving dropped boxes, tripping up, etc., until the Princess runs back in wailing.

PRINCESS   Oh! Oh! Oh!

TWANKY   What's up with her? Sounds like someone's stepped on *her* bunions!

PRINCESS   Oh! Oh! Oh!

ALADDIN   What's the matter, my darling, my pretty
                one, my Princess?

PRINCESS   Oh! Oh! Oh!

Enter Anakadin with the lamp.

ALADDIN   Oh! Oh! Oh!

TWANKY   Oh! Oh! Oh!

ALL THREE   Oh! Oh! Oh!

ANAKADIN   Yes! Oh! Oh! Oh! Indeed! Ha, ha, ha, ha!

Aladdin suddenly has a brainwave.

ALADDIN   *(to the audience)* I still have the magic ring
                the magician gave me when I was a boy.
                (shows the ring and rubs it vigorously)

Enter the Genie of the Ring, yawning and rubbing his eyes.

GENIE   Oh Master, you've disturbed me. I was just in
                the middle of a lovely dream about a . . .

ALADDIN   Never mind that now! I wish . . .

*Anakadin realizes what's going on and starts to rub the lamp,
but Widow Twanky at the same moment trips over her feet and
falls headlong into Anakadin, knocking him to the ground,
showering him with her shoe boxes and sending the lamp flying
to the other side of the stage.*

ALADDIN   Oh, well done, Mother! Now just hold him
                there for a moment!

Widow Twanky pins Anakadin to the floor.

ALADDIN Now . . . Genie! I wish that . . . *(to the audience)* Shall I wish that he dies a nasty death? *(encourages audience to reply)* No? Shall I wish that he sits for ever in a bath of ice cubes? *(encourages audience to reply)* No? Shall I wish that he has to travel everywhere by train in rush hour for the rest of his life? *(encourages audience to reply)* No? I know! My mother has been terribly lonely since my father died. Genie, I wish that you would turn Anakadin into a perfect husband for my mother, Widow Twanky, and that he never again has any nasty thoughts about me, the Princess or the lamp!

GENIE Your wish is my command, O Master!

Genie performs suitable arm movements and Anakadin sits up.

ANAKADIN Oh, Madam! Beautiful, fair madam! Have you dropped all your boxes? Allow me to assist.

Anakadin and Widow Twanky gather the boxes up from all over the floor and pile them neatly at the side of the stage, link arms and gaze into each other's eyes. Enter the Narrator. Aladdin, the Princess and the Narrator all encourage the audience to say 'Ahhhhhhhh'.

NARRATOR And they all lived happily ever after!

Cast bow. Exit.

Football Final/Sports Event

Introduction

This section provides ideas related to football, although most could be translated to fit other team sports. If your church is not the energetic type, you could still use the two talks provided for outreach-focused Sunday services around the time of major sporting events such as the UEFA Cup or the Olympics.

26. Big Screen Event

If your church has a video projector and screen, why not show key sports events and provide refreshments? If your church does not have the equipment, it is available to hire (check your *Yellow Pages*).

You could screen the event purely as a bridge-builder, or you could include an evangelistic talk. Decide for yourself which of the two talks provided in this section would be best for your audience.

27. Talk: 'Football and the Game of Life'

Opening illustration

The worst recorded soccer match was in 1973. Oxbarn Social Club football team arranged a friendly match in Germany. It was an opportunity for the lads who played in the Wolverhampton Sunday League to get a holiday abroad and also for them to meet some new opposition. Only when they had entered their opponents' luxury stadium did they realize that they had in fact mistakenly arranged a friendly with top German first division side, SVW Mainz. SVW Mainz were expecting to play Wolverhampton Wanderers, one of the strongest teams in Britain at that time. The Oxbarn Club secretary said, 'I thought it looked posh, and when I heard the other side were on an £80 bonus to win, I said to myself, "Something is wrong."' After the fifteenth goal whistled into Oxbarn's net, their goalkeeper was seen to fall onto his knees. He seemed to be praying for the final whistle. It was around this time that the sixteenth and seventeenth goals were scored. Oxbarn Social Club lost 21–0.

Football is very much like life. If life is a game, then what are the rules?

Point 1 (sin): It's a game of two halves

What you do with God in the first half (before you die) will determine what God does with you in the second (after you die). Most people do not want anything to do with God in the first half. We were created to play by God's rules. When we don't play by God's rules we sin.

(Bible verse: Romans 2:6) God will give to each person according to what he has done.

Point 2 (forgiveness): Time to make a substitute

To use a substitute can be disheartening in a match, but one is needed if none of the players is scoring in the first half.

(Bible verse: Romans 3:23) For all have sinned and fall short of the glory of God.

Players can easily blame a bad cross or a bad tackle for their missing the goal. We are all missing the goal of perfection that God demands. This is our own doing and no one else's. We cannot blame anyone or anything else. We miss this goal because we do not allow God into our lives. If God were to rescue us he would have to make a substitution.

(Bible verse: 2 Corinthians 5:21) God made him who had no sin to be sin for us.

Our sin needs to be punished, but Jesus became our substitute. Instead of God punishing us, Jesus quite literally took the punishment for us. He died in our place and God can forgive us because he substituted Jesus for us.

Point 3 (response): God wants you on his team

A free transfer is on offer for you to leave and sign up to God.

(Bible verse: 1 Samuel 16:7) Man looks on the outward appearance, but the LORD looks at the heart.

It's not about what you are worth or what you can do for God. It's all about what he has already done for you.

- **Admit** to God and yourself that you have sinned; that you have left God out of your life and gone your own way.
- **Believe** that Jesus came to this world to die on the cross to take your punishment so that you could be forgiven.
- **Commit** your whole life to God. Turn away from living life your way and start living it God's way.

Do this and mean it, and God will forgive you.

28. Awards Ceremony and Meal for Football Team

Some churches have football teams that play in local church leagues. The teams usually have a mix of Christian and non-Christian players. Inviting non-Christian friends to join the team or come to practices is a great way of getting them involved with your church. Why not find out whether you have a local church league and start a team (not forgetting to invite work colleagues, neighbours and other non-Christian contacts to join)? You might be surprised how keen other churches are to join you or to put forward their own team! Don't limit your ideas to adult male football teams! If there is enough interest, youth teams or women's teams are also possibilities. And if your church isn't interested in football, how about setting up a rounders league, squash ladder, cycling club or rambling club?

At the end of the season, hold an awards ceremony and meal. Encourage players to bring their partners. The meal could be held in a local function room or at your church if you have suitable facilities and a catering team. Enjoy the meal and awards, but use the opportunity to give a themed evangelistic talk, like the ones outlined in this section. It is commonplace to listen to an after-dinner talk at events like these.

29. Football Five-a-Side Tournament

As mentioned in the previous idea, sport provides a great opportunity to build bridges between the church and those outside. If the idea of starting a regular football event seems too large a task, why not hold a five-a-side football tournament instead? Again you should use the opportunity to invite work colleagues, neighbours and so on to join your team or field their own.

Encourage the players to bring their families. Advertise in local shops and maybe in the local press. You could hire a bouncy castle and run a 'coffee shop' with a few tables and chairs, and an exhibition about your church and the activities it runs.

At the end of the day hold an awards ceremony preceded by a brief evangelistic talk, as outlined in Idea 30.

30. Talk: 'The Greatest Commentator'

Opening illustration

There have been many commentators who, in their haste to report how they saw the game, did not make much sense.

Murray Walker: 'Rally points scoring is 20 points for the fastest, 18 points for the second fastest, right down to 6 points for the slowest fastest.'

Des Lynam: 'Born in Italy, most of his fights have been in his native New York.'

Steve Brenkley: 'Alderman knows he's either going to get a wicket or he's not.'

Richie Benaud: 'His throw went absolutely nowhere near where it was going.'

Brendan Foster: 'The Kenyans haven't done much in the last two Olympic games – in fact they haven't competed.'

Dave Coleman: 'The Republic of China is back in the Olympic games for the first time.'

Nigel Smith: 'Britain's last gold medal was a bronze in 1952 in Helsinki.'

Point 1 (sin): God sees your life

Like the best commentator, God sees everything, and that includes us. God sees all our pain, all our suffering, all our regrets, all our sorrows, all our mistakes. However, unlike many commentators as illustrated in the opening quotes, he does not make any mistakes. God sees our wrong but still cares for us and wants to forgive us!

(Bible verses: Psalm 139:1–4) O LORD, you have searched me and you know me. You know when I sit and when I rise; you perceive my thoughts from afar. You discern my going out and my lying down; you are familiar with all my ways. Before a word is on my tongue you know it completely, O LORD.

Point 2 (forgiveness and response): God wants to change what he sees

God is the great commentator, but he also wants to be your coach, physio and manager. He wants to train you and heal you and lead you into what is best for your life, but you must trust him in what he asks you to do.

(Bible verses: Proverbs 3:5–7) Trust in the LORD with all your heart and lean not on your own understanding; in all your ways acknowledge him, and he will make your paths straight. Do not be wise in your own eyes; fear the LORD and shun evil.

God wants to forgive us our mistakes. He allowed his own Son Jesus to die on a cross to make this possible. Now he asks you to do the following:

• **Admit** to God and yourself that you have sinned; that you have left God out of your life and gone your own way.

- **B**elieve that Jesus came to this world to die on the cross to take your punishment so that you could be forgiven.
- Commit your whole life to God. Turn away from living life your way and start living it God's way.

Accept and believe what God sees and says of your life. In doing this and meaning it God will forgive you.

Summer Holiday

Introduction

The summer holidays are a strange time in the church year: many people are away and those who aren't have children around with six weeks off school. Because of this, events can be either very badly attended or very well attended, and it is difficult to foresee which will be the case. Nevertheless, it is worth holding a fun summer holiday event, and if it is a great success people will make sure they can attend the following year. If you intend people to queue for refreshments, erect a church publicity stand next to the queue, detailing future events and weekly meetings (e.g. youth group, mums and toddlers, men's breakfast, etc.).

31. Talk: 'Stop! Are You on the Right Track?'

Opening illustration

Have you ever suddenly realized you were going the wrong way in your car and stopped to ask for directions? If so, have you ever been told by the person giving directions, 'If I were you, I wouldn't start from here'?

I want to show you how to get on the right track in life.

Point 1 (sin): God's way

Scientist Albert Einstein said, 'I want to know God's thoughts. The rest are details.'

God's way is the best way. Because he made us, he alone knows how we are most fulfilled. You need to know what God's thoughts for your life are. Everything else is just details.

(Bible verse: Isaiah 48:17) I am the LORD your God, who teaches you what is best for you, who directs you in the way you should go.

The problem is that we say, 'I want to go my way,' but is the way we live our life really working? God is not against you, but he is against the way you are going.

If we have no place for God in our lives, the Bible calls this sin, which needs to be punished.

Point 2 (forgiveness): Only way

Did you know that only Jesus can get you to God? Tennis star Michael Chang said, 'The money's great but it won't last. What will last is the love of Christ in my heart.' Jesus Christ is the only way to lasting fulfilment, but more importantly he is the only way to God. He is the only way to the only way.

(Bible verse: John 14:6) Jesus answered, 'I am the way and the truth and the life. No-one comes to the Father but by me.'

God allows no other way because our forgiveness cost him his only Son. Jesus died willingly, the difference being it was for our mistakes, not his. People say you can come to God however you want. After all, all roads lead to Rome. The problem is, God does not live in Rome.

Point 3 (response): Turn away

If you were on a journey and you realized that you were going the wrong way, you would be foolish to keep on going that way.

(Bible verse: Luke 13:3) Unless you repent, you too will all perish.

- Admit to God that you have lived your life your way and not his way.
- Believe that Jesus died on the cross, taking the punishment for our wrong.
- Commit your life to God and living life his way.

Do this and mean it, and God will forgive you.

32. Treasure Hunt Car Rally

A summer treasure hunt or scavenger hunt on foot is always popular with families, teens, students and young couples. Make it even more exciting by combining the hunt with a car rally. The hunt/rally should last between 1 and 1½ hours. Aim to meet at the end for a communal picnic or barbecue, as this will encourage church members to socialize with guests and provide an opportunity for a brief evangelistic address and prizegiving ceremony. (The talk provided in this section has an appropriate theme.)

Establish a set of rules and hand them out to each team before they start the treasure hunt (e.g. keep to the speed limit, safety belts must be worn while the vehicle is moving).

Scavenger hunt

A scavenger hunt requires the teams to collect items from a list or acquire information within a specified time limit. With today's technology, the traditional scavenger hunt could be updated to use digital photographs or a video diary to prove that tasks were accomplished. (If used with youth, students or young couples this could provide fun viewing at a future event, giving an opportunity to invite your guests again.)

Examples of items to collect:
- A hard-boiled egg
- An information booklet on a local landmark (e.g. castle)
- Five daisies

149

- Something pink
- A feather

The list should be a mixture of hard and easy items. Ensure that you have enough items to keep the teams busy for at least one hour.

Examples of information to acquire:

- In what year was such and such a building built?
- Who was the mayor in such and such a year?
- Who are the local cricket club playing next week?
- What colour are the doors of the local library?
- What type of tree is growing next door to the police station?

A visit to the Tourist Information office for your town will provide you with plenty of ideas. Look for information that can be obtained by finding plaques on buildings, signs, etc. as well as information available at the local library or Tourist Information office.

Examples of photo or video tasks:

- Introduce yourself to a six-foot blonde
- Kiss an elephant
- Sing in a pop band
- Survey what ministers like best for Sunday lunch
- See if eight out of ten cats do prefer Whiskas

Teams should be encouraged to use not only their initiative but also their imagination (e.g. kissing a toy elephant). It will probably be necessary to extend the hunt over a full afternoon or day in order that a number of tasks can be attempted.

Treasure hunt

There are various ways of running a treasure hunt, but whichever way you choose it is important to stagger the teams and judge the winner on fastest time to prevent competitors from all following one another.

A treasure hunt can take the form of a 'single leg journey', where directions are given in clue format for the entire journey between two points.

The alternative is to set up manned checkpoints along the route and to provide the team with a map and the first checkpoint clue. The next clue is picked up at the first checkpoint and so on. The clues merely identify the location of the next checkpoint – how the teams reach the checkpoint is down to them and their map-reading and route-planning skills.

Some suggestions for different styles of clue are listed below:

Cryptic clues

Remember Anneka Rice and *Treasure Hunt* in the 1980s, or the famously hard *Masquerade* treasure trove book by Kit Williams? Well, here's your chance to have a go . . .

Cryptic Journey: give instructions to the finish line via cryptic directions (e.g. turn the correct way at the aged monarch and proceed for half a millennium until you reach the refreshments junction = turn right at the Queen Vic and proceed for 500 metres until you reach the T junction). Use your own imagination to think up the cryptic directions, or try giving the directions in story form or in cockney rhyming slang. This takes a long time to plan as every step of the route has to be noted and converted into a cryptic clue, and you must ensure that the rally takes at least an hour to make the event worthwhile.

Checkpoint Clues: provide each team with a map and maybe a tourist guide of the area. Start each team off with a cryptic clue to get them to the first checkpoint, where they will receive their next clue. Unravelling the cryptic clue reveals the location of the checkpoint (maybe requiring reference to the tourist guide) and then it's up to the teams to make their way to the checkpoint using the map and asking for directions. A visit to the Tourist Information office will provide you with plenty of material, along with free or cheap guides. If you're really clever, write the clues in rhyming verse.

Map grid co-ordinates

The clues could take the format of precise grid co-ordinates for each checkpoint using Eastings and Northings, along with a copy of a suitably gridded map (e.g. Ordnance Survey Landranger Series is in 1:50,000, where each grid square equals 1000 m and each millimetre equals 50 m). Also provide an instruction sheet on how to translate grid co-ordinates into map position (e.g. 407450 E, 458750 N).

Photo clues

Provide a photo for each clue. The photo could be of either a well-known landmark or an unusual feature (like an unusual door or piece of architecture) accompanied by an extra clue to get the teams into the general vicinity. The website at www.multimap.co.uk features aerial photos and historic photos of some areas, which may provide an interesting alternative, or you could take 'view from checkpoint' photos and let the teams guess where the photo would have been taken from. Another slant would be to take photos at major points along the journey to act as sole clues to reach the checkpoint (e.g. interesting houses, unusual trees, road signs, major junctions).

Harvest

Introduction

In rural churches, Harvest Festival is still celebrated with special services and suppers that are inclusive of all members of the community, regardless of whether they are regular church attenders. By contrast, there is a tendency among some urban churches to give harvest celebrations a miss, as they are deemed irrelevant. The celebration of harvest gives us an opportunity not only to thank God for his provision, but also to involve our local community in our church family.

If you decide to hold a Harvest Supper, why not use the format of the International Evening suggested earlier in this book? A lot of the food we eat in Britain is imported from other countries, so try serving a menu that reflects the dishes of the country that grows the foodstuff (e.g. canned tomatoes and pasta produced in Italy used to make lasagne, lentils from Turkey used in Turkish lentil soup, and rice from India used in a biryani). You could also lay out a table of foodstuffs from around the world and hold a competition to see which team can guess which countries the items come from.

33. Talk: 'A Time for Giving'

Do you ever suffer from supermarket stress? This is the kind of stress you get when people insist on having a conversation right in the middle of the aisle; the stress you get from too many options; the stress you get when you seem to have picked the trolley with the dodgy wheel; the stress you get when you end up with the slow checkout operator. All that said, where would we be without Sainsbury, Tesco, Safeway or Asda? Somehow the convenience of a supermarket far outweighs the stress it causes. It's better than having to farm the food ourselves. Somehow we forget the significance of food provision because it's all done for us. Part of being grateful is giving to those who don't have what we have.

Point 1 (sin): God is for giving

Picture the scene: children with their fruit baskets, bags of vegetables or boxes of dried fruit walking down the school or church aisle to the song 'All good gifts around us are sent from heaven above'. Let's remember that it has little to do with Mr Sainsbury as to whether we get our food, but it is all down to God. Be happy that God is 'for giving' (i.e. pro giving). He loves to give us much more than we are often willing to receive.

(Bible verse: John 10:28) I give them eternal life, and they shall never perish; no-one can snatch them out of my hand.

God wants to give each one of us eternal life. That means quantity and quality of life. God gave his own Son Jesus

155

because we often don't give our lives to him. We keep our lives out of God's hands. This stops us knowing God and enjoying what he has to offer.

Point 2 (forgiveness): God is forgiving

(Bible verse: Matthew 20:28) The Son of Man did not come to be served, but to serve, and to give his life as a ransom for many.

God gave Jesus even though we didn't deserve it. Jesus willingly came as a gift to humankind. While he walked the earth, he constantly gave of himself. The greatest demonstration of his willingness to serve and give was in giving his life for us.

(Bible verse: John 10:18) No-one takes it from me, but I lay it down of my own accord.

Jesus willingly gave his life to show that God is not only *for giving* but is *forgiving*. God gave Jesus and Jesus gave his life so that we could be forgiven by God. God demanded death for our wrong and Jesus was willing to give his life for us. Jesus came back to life and gives new life to each one of us.

Point 3 (response): Are you for giving?

(Bible verse: John 3:16) For God so loved the world that he gave his one and only Son, that whoever believes in him shall not perish but have eternal life.

If you give your life to Jesus, you can receive all that God wants to give you.

• **Admit to God and yourself that you have sinned; that you have left God out of your life and gone your own way.**

- **B**elieve that Jesus came to this world to die on the cross to take your punishment so that you can be forgiven.
- **C**ommit your whole life to God. Turn away from living life your way and start living it God's way.

Give your life to God and mean what you are doing, and you will receive God's forgiveness and all that he wants to give to you.

34. Harvest Festival Collection 'Jewish Style'

The Feast of Tabernacles (or Sukkot) is celebrated by the Jewish community during our autumn months. It lasts for about nine days and is held to commemorate the time when the Israelites wandered in the desert for forty years living only in huts (*sukkot*). The festival starts at sundown five days after Yom Kippur with the blowing of a *shofar* (ram's horn). The festival relates to an instruction in Leviticus:

(Bible verses: Leviticus 23:42–43) Live in booths for seven days . . . so that your descendants will know that I made the Israelites live in booths when I brought them out of Egypt. I am the LORD your God.

The celebrations involve erecting a temporary shelter (*sukkah* or tabernacle) and living in it for seven days, though these days most merely eat in the *sukkot*. The *sukkot* are covered with foliage and the insides are decorated with fruit and vegetables (e.g. apples, grapes, pomegranates). Another important part of the celebrations is hospitality and the sharing of meals with others, and because of this the festival is also called the Festival of the Ingathering.

The start dates for the Feast of Tabernacles over the next three years are as follows:

10th October 2003 (sundown)
29th September 2004 (sundown)
17th October 2005 (sundown)

More information can be found at www.holidays.net/sukkot.

Add a different slant to your Harvest Service and erect a *sukkah* in the church and decorate it with foliage and harvest fare. Explain to the congregation about the Feast of Tabernacles and remind them of the story in Exodus when God led the Israelites around the desert for forty years before bringing them to 'the land of milk and honey'. Take time to reflect upon the fragility of life and material possessions, and our dependence upon God to sustain the earth. Give thanks to God for his faithfulness in sustaining our life on earth and for his promise of an eternal 'land of milk and honey' when we die.

After the blowing of a horn (or a *shofar* if you can get hold of one), ask the children to process to the *sukkah* with their gifts of canned and dried food as their way of offering hospitality to others. Inform the church of the intended recipients of the food, perhaps a local charity for the homeless. Place a bucket in the *sukkah* and give the adults a chance to donate money if they wish to.

All Saints' Day
(Alternative Halloween)

Introduction

Whether we like it or not, Halloween is an established annual institution. Young people in particular will unavoidably come into contact with this celebration on 31st October and be under pressure from peers to take part both at school and at social events. Providing an alternative Halloween at your church will help them and their friends to have a fun evening, while avoiding the perhaps unsavoury and unsafe aspects.

Halloween appears to have originated from an amalgamation of pagan customs, in particular the Celtic New Year celebration, Samhain; the Roman festival of the dead, Feralia; and the Roman festival of the harvest, Pomona. In the seventh century, Pope Boniface IV instituted All Saints' Day to replace Samhain, Feralia and other similar pagan festivals in the Christian world, to discourage the practices of sacrificing and offering prayers to the dead and instead provide an opportunity to remember the dead before God. All Saints' Day became a major festival in the Catholic Church, so the night before became a vigil, hence All Hallows' (Saints') Eve or Halloween.

35. Talk: 'Trick or Treat?'

Opening illustration

- Trick or treat? Halloween is the night when kids are encouraged to talk to strangers and get things from them, when we discourage it during the rest of the year.
- Trick or treat? Halloween is the night when kids dress up and make a joke of what is serious.
- Trick or treat? Halloween is the night when you get a trick played on you unless you give a treat.

Point 1 (sin): Trick!

We have been tricked. A trick makes you believe something is happening when it isn't. (Tell in your own words the story of how Satan tricked Adam and Eve: Genesis 3:1–6. Point out Satan's initial attempt to confuse by asking, 'You must not eat from any tree?' followed by the blatant lie in verse 4, 'You will not surely die.')

(Bible verse: Genesis 3:13) Then the LORD God said to the woman, 'What is this you have done?' The woman said, 'The serpent deceived me, and I ate.'

The truth is, we ourselves continue to allow ourselves to be tricked every day about many things, e.g. about what is right and wrong, about the existence of God, about the importance of preparing for the afterlife and about how we can gain forgiveness and eternal life.

We have tricked ourselves. We say, 'I don't need God.' We believe that we can remain uninterested in God and just try to 'be good' and that we will still get into heaven when we die. The truth is, there is no sitting on the fence. God says we are either on his side or else we are on the other side. There is no middle ground. Make sure you are on God's side.

Point 2 (forgiveness): Treat!

We get what we don't deserve. God has treated us (i.e. given us something nice that we haven't earned), and treated us (i.e. dealt with us) all the same.

(Bible verses: Ephesians 2:8–9) For it is by grace you have been saved, through faith – and this is not from yourselves, it is the gift of God – not by works, so that no-one can boast.

Explain the verses: *It is by [God's] grace* (his undeserved loving kindness) *you have been saved* (rescued from the effects of sin in this life and the afterlife), *through faith* (by actively believing in God) – *and this is not from yourselves* (you can't earn it), *it is the gift of God* (God's treat that we don't deserve).

(Bible verse: Romans 6:23) The wages of sin is death, but the gift of God is eternal life in Christ Jesus our Lord.

We don't get what we *do* deserve. We deserve to suffer the consequences of our sin (i.e. separation from God and his favour, both in this world and the next), but Jesus took the punishment (the wages of our sin) for us. We get treated because Jesus was mistreated.

Talk about how Jesus was mistreated, his crucifixion and the hours leading up to it (see John 18–19; Luke 22–23; Mark 14–15; Matthew 26–27).

Point 3 (response): Trick or treat?

Will you stay tricked or will you accept God's treat? To get God's 'treat' of forgiveness and new life:

- Admit to God and yourself that you have sinned; that you have left God out of your life and gone your own way.
- Believe that Jesus came to this world to die on the cross to take your punishment so that you could be forgiven.
- Commit your whole life to God. Turn away from living life your way and start living it God's way.

Do this and mean it, and God will treat you by forgiving you.

36. Seasonal Games

The following is a list of suggestions for a number of seasonal (but religiously sensitive) games for all ages. They could be used at an alternative Halloween family or youth event. (Some game ideas have been taken from www.gamekids.com.)

Apple bobbing and variations

The traditional Halloween game is apple bobbing. A number of apples are floated in a bowl of water and participants must attempt to get an apple out of the water using only their mouths (hands behind backs). The result is that everyone gets very wet! There are many other variations on this theme, most to do with extracting an item in a messy or unpleasant fashion. They include ring doughnuts or peeled bananas suspended on strings – the winner is the first to eat the item with their hands behind their backs without it falling on the floor; marbles or grapes in bowls of ice cubes to be extracted with one's toes; marshmallows floating in a bowl to be extracted by suction using a straw; balloons containing charades and sweets: the balloon must be burst and then the charade acted out – the person to guess the charade gets the sweet and must burst the next balloon.

Dressing up and variations

Dressing up is a common theme at Halloween and although traditional costumes may not be thought appropriate for a

Christian celebration, many people still wish to dress up. The following games help compensate for this.

Scarecrow relay

You will need two sacks full of old clothes (e.g. shirt, overalls, gloves, oversized boots/shoes, hat, pipe, neck scarf – but each sack needs to contain the same number of items). Divide into two teams. Each team must choose one person to be their 'scarecrow'. This is a relay race: each member of the team in turn must delve into the sack, pull out an item of clothing and then run to their 'scarecrow' (who is standing at the end of the room) and dress them in the item of clothing. They then return to tag the next team member. The first team to have an empty sack and all the items on the scarecrow is the winner.

Chilly chocolate relay

You will need two scarves, two woolly hats, two pairs of large cumbersome gloves, two sets of knives and forks, two plastic plates and two large bars of chocolate. Set out two lanes for the race. At the end of each lane place a wrapped bar of chocolate on a plastic plate and lay out a knife and fork, then leave items of winter clothing at intervals down each lane. Divide into two teams. This is a relay race: each member of the team in turn must run to the end of the lane putting on the items of winter clothing as they go. When they reach the chocolate they must cut and eat one piece of chocolate using the knife and fork (the first team member must unwrap the bar with the knife and fork). They then return to tag the next team member, taking off the items of clothing as they return and leaving them where they found them. The first team to have had every member run is the winner.

Farmer John relay

You will need two large sacks. In each sack put boxer shorts, trousers, big long socks, shirt, jumper, crazy wig, hat, etc., and place at the end of the room. Divide into two teams. This is a relay race: each member of the team in turn must run to their team's sack, put on Farmer John's entire wardrobe over what they are already wearing and then model it for five seconds, then take everything off, put it back in the sack and run back to tag the next member. The first team to have had every member run is the winner.

Pumpkin games

The following games involve using a pumpkin instead of a ball to give the game a seasonal twist. Try pumpkin bowling with a small round pumpkin. If you don't have skittles, use ten washing-up liquid bottles filled with three inches of water and resealed.

Or try 'Pumpkin Toss', similar to Egg Toss but replacing the egg with a small pumpkin. Two people toss the pumpkin back and forth to each other, each time taking a step backwards to move further away from each other. The winner is the one who does not drop the pumpkin.

'Pumpkin Puzzle' is a 3D jigsaw. Cut the lid off two pumpkins and clean out the middle, then cut each pumpkin into puzzle pieces. Each team is given the pieces to their pumpkin and a jar of cocktail sticks. The first team to reassemble their pumpkin is the winner.

Spider's web

Everyone stands in a circle and each participant is given a small ball of black wool. Everyone ties the end of their wool around their waist and then the first player tosses their ball to someone across the circle, who then wraps that ball around their waist, keeping that ball before tossing their own ball to someone else across the circle. A spider's web evolves and once it is deemed that the web is complex enough the game can in theory stop, although most of the fun comes from trying to untangle the players afterwards. Have scissors handy!

Black light face painting and decorations

You may decide that the sorts of request for face painting that are inevitable on a Halloween night preclude offering this activity. However, if you are able to get hold of black light equipment there will be novelty in merely being painted with designs. When the lights are turned off and the black lights turned on, the room will be filled with lots of glowing hands and faces. Inevitably, adults will want to play too! Disco and stage lighting suppliers can provide black light equipment (UV lighting) for sale or hire, and theatrical make-up companies should be able to provide water-based UV face paints (suppliers Fardel and Kryolan). Try a company called Screen Face in London (order online at www.screenface.com or telephone and place a mail order). It is also possible to get black light decorations and silly string. And even black light puppets (from www.onewayuk.com)!

37. Quiz

The following list of saints could be handed out on a sheet of paper (without the answers). Each team has to write down the thing that each patron saint is most commonly associated with. Tell them to use their common sense and guess for some of them. Give a prize to the team with the most correct answers. Most saints are patrons of a great deal of things, so other less common answers are given in brackets after the main answer.

1. St Cecilia – musicians
2. St Christopher – travellers
3. St David – Wales (poets)
4. St Crispin – cobblers
5. St Gabriel – messengers (postal workers/broadcasters/radio workers)
6. St Michael – grocers (police officers/battle)
7. St Matthew – accountants
8. St Luke – surgeons (physicians/artists/painters/glassworkers)
9. St Andrew – Scotland (fishermen)
10. St Sebastian – athletes
11. St Ambrose – bee keeping (learning)
12. St Stephen – bricklayers
13. St Valentine – lovers
14. St Barbara – architects
15. St Vitus – dancers (comedians/actors)
16. St Joseph – carpenters (social justice/fathers/dying/church)

17. St Joseph of Arimathea – funeral directors
18. St Thomas – doubters
19. St George – England
20. St Patrick – Ireland

Bonfire Night

Introduction

The 5th November is celebrated throughout Britain with fireworks and bonfires. Loud bangs and smoke fill the air in the week or so running up to this night. People of all ages, but especially those with children, plan to celebrate either by attending a display or by hosting their own in their back garden. Many feel that the large public displays are impersonal and that the crowds and parking are a nuisance, but also see no alternative, as they are unhappy to risk fireworks and a bonfire in their own garden. Pubs, schools and other hubs of the local community often host smaller, more intimate displays, and the church can be seen to fit into this group of those hosting local community events.

38. Talk: 'Remember, Remember, the Fifth of November!'

Opening illustration

The most unsuccessful firework ever ignited was the Fat Man Roman Candle perfected in 1975 by Mr George Plimton of New York. It weighed 720 pounds, measured 40 inches in length and was developed to break the record for the most spectacular firework ever. Lighting it, Mr Plimton confidently predicted that it would reach an altitude in excess of 3,000 feet. Instead of this, however, it hissed, whistled and blew a 10 foot crater in the earth!

How many times are fireworks disappointing? God doesn't want our life to be disappointing; he wants our life to be full of promise and fulfilment.

There are things that we remember on bonfire night:

Point 1 (sin): Remember the Fireworks Code

The slogan used in a TV ad in 1997 was, 'This bonfire night, throw a party, throw a wobbly, but don't throw a firework.' This was due to the fact that in 1996 there had been 12,000 injuries caused by 5th November festivities.

It is fun at this point to ask people if they know the Fireworks Code.

Do

1. keep fireworks in a closed box
2. follow instructions on each firework
3. light fireworks at arm's length

175

4. stay well back
5. wear gloves – even sparklers get and stay very hot

Don't

1. use a naked flame – use a taper
2. go back to a firework once lit – it may go off in your face
3. keep fireworks in a pocket
4. put pets out
5. throw or fool around with fireworks. It is an offence to throw fireworks in a public place. (Fine = £5,000)

This code is not intended to ruin bonfire night; it is there so all can enjoy it.

God has given us a code of ten things. We often refer to it as the Ten Commandments, but I like to call it the Lifeworks Code because if you follow it, *life works*. It is not there to ruin your life; it is there so that you can enjoy life and please God at the same time.

(Bible verse: Leviticus 18:5) Keep my decrees and laws, for the man who obeys them will live by them.

God's decrees and laws are positive, not negative. Laws are there to benefit society. God's laws were intended for benefit, never for deficit. If we don't live by God's standards and don't obey his rules, we cannot have a friendship with him.

Point 2 (forgiveness): Remember the punishment

Guy Fawkes was punished for trying to blow up the Houses of Parliament. He was punished for what he had done. Do not just remember the punishment of someone who deserved what he got, but also remember the punishment of someone who got what he did not deserve. Jesus Christ was punished for our crime.

(Bible verse: 2 Corinthians 5:21) God made him who had no sin to be sin for us.

Jesus never did anything wrong, but he took the punishment for our wrong on the cross.

Point 3 (response): Remember not to forget

Remember not to forget to respond to what you have heard tonight. It's easy for us to hear something challenging and then go away and forget about it.

* **A**dmit to God and yourself that you have sinned; that you have left God out of your life and gone your own way.
* **B**elieve that Jesus came to this world to die on the cross to take your punishment so that you could be forgiven.
* **C**ommit your whole life to God. Turn away from living life your way and start living it God's way.

Do this and mean it, and God will forgive you.

39. Talk: 'Say It with Fireworks'

Opening illustration

Does anyone know what temperature a firework burns at? Well, a simple sparkler reaches a temperature of up to 2,000°C. That's twenty times the boiling point of water. How fast does a firework travel? Typically a rocket can reach 150 miles an hour. And how high can a firework go? Well, a shell fired from a mortar will go as high as 200 metres. The largest ever single firework was a shell that measured one metre across and travelled over 300 metres into the air. It was so big and powerful it had to be launched from a specially constructed launch pad made of concrete and steel. The record for the biggest number of rockets ever let off in one go was set at the Battle of Flowers Moonlight Parade in Jersey on 15th August 1997, when a staggering 39,210 rockets were simultaneously launched at the push of a button.

The French celebrate the French Revolution of 1789 and the storming of the Bastille on 14th July with parties, parades and fireworks. In Northern Ireland fireworks are used to celebrate Halloween. The Jews often celebrate Hanukkah with fireworks around December or January. Many Asians celebrate Diwali, a festival of light, in the last week of October or the first week of November. Candles and fireworks and the exchanging of gifts are important parts of this festival. In Canada, they even hold an annual World Fireworks Championship.

Fireworks were invented over 2,000 years ago in China. Many countries use fireworks for different celebrations to remind people of important things – in fact it's almost as if they, 'Say it with fireworks.'

Point 1 (sin): USA says 'Independence!'

American Independence Day (4th July) celebrates the signing of the Declaration of Independence. There are parades, and people hold street parties and put on firework displays.

(Bible verses: Proverbs 3:5–7) Trust in the LORD with all your heart and lean not on your own understanding; in all your ways acknowledge him, and he will make your paths straight. Do not be wise in your own eyes; fear the LORD and shun evil.

Don't live independently of God. Sin is all the wrong things we do, say and think. In particular it is leaving God out of our lives, living independently of him. When we don't put God first, we sin. Don't leave God out of your life. Turn away from wrong and trust in him. Let him guide your life.

Point 2 (forgiveness): China says 'Keep evil away!'

In China, the New Year falls about a month after our own and involves a fortnight-long celebration. There is an outdoor festival of lanterns, and firecrackers are let off to scare away evil spirits. In the Lord's Prayer, Jesus said that we should pray to God, our Father, in the following way:

(Bible verses: Matthew 6:12–13) 'Forgive us our debts [sins] as we also have forgiven our debtors [those who sin against us] . . . deliver us from the evil one . . .'

Only God can protect us from evil. Only God can and will forgive our sins: our evil thoughts, words and deeds.

Point 3 (response): Germany says 'A new start!'

In Germany, people traditionally let off fireworks on New Year's Eve. The skies are lit up from midnight, well into the early hours of the morning. On the dawning of the millennium, Sydney (Australia) spent £3 million on fireworks. In fifteen minutes the UK sent 40,000 fireworks into the night sky of London to say welcome to the year 2000. The display was so spectacular that it could be seen from outer space.

(Bible verse: Romans 6:4) Just as Christ was raised from the dead through the glory of the Father, we too may have new life.

We are all guilty of living independently of God, as well as doing, saying and thinking wrong things. But God is able to forgive us and give us a fresh start because Jesus took the punishment for our wrong on the cross. What you need to do is:

- **A**dmit to God and yourself that you have sinned; that you have left God out of your life and live independently of him.
- **B**elieve that Jesus came to this world to die on the cross to take your punishment so that you could be forgiven.
- **C**ommit your whole life to God. Turn away from living life your way and start afresh, living it God's way.

Do this and mean it, and God will forgive you.

40. Firework/Bonfire Party

Hold a church-organized firework/bonfire party. With good advertising this will attract a lot of guests, including the possibility of completely new contacts if it promises to be a good display and is free! Start early (6.30 pm is an acceptable time) as young children will be attending. Holding the event on the closest Saturday to 5th November is a popular date and will allow the early start required and 'late' night without school the next morning.

Strategy 1: Pre-evangelism event

A fireworks display would work well as 'pre-evangelism' and could attract new contacts. As well as the usual encouragement to church members to bring their friends, put an additional emphasis on reaching completely new people. Produce a large number of flyers (A5 handouts) and leaflet-drop your local area/community a couple of weeks before the event. Ask local shops to display posters, and if your church has links with local nurseries and schools ask them to advertise the event if they are not holding their own. Put up a large eye-catching poster advertising the event on your outside church noticeboard. If you have children's clubs running at your church, hand out the flyers with a covering letter for the kids to take home to their parents. Stipulation of a minimum 'unsupervised' age will help with safety and will also encourage non-Christian parents to attend the event.

As there is to be no evangelistic address at this event, you must ensure that it is as successful as possible in terms of bridge-building. Instruct your church members beforehand about being outward-looking and friendly at the event. Ensure that you have a display about your church and the activities it runs by the food stall queue (if outside make sure that it is well lit!). Also plan your next evangelistic outreach event in advance and have flyers prepared and available at the display. Maybe those manning the food stall could give out a flyer with each napkin. If you have means of voice amplification, announce the next event during a break in the fireworks and inform listeners of where to pick up a flyer. Do not leave this until the end, as many people do not stay right through due to the cold, especially if they have small children.

Strategy 2: 'Light' evangelistic event

An alternative option is to aim for smaller numbers, perhaps concentrating on those with whom the church already has some contact, and include a short topical evangelistic address during the evening's events. Church members should be encouraged to invite their friends, relatives and work colleagues; and parents of children attending kids' clubs should be invited to attend with their children. Also invite people who have attended previous outreach events, and 'fringe members' who attend church infrequently or who have stopped coming altogether. Think carefully through all the church's contacts with the community: mums and tots, luncheon club, any groups that use the church hall or have some contact with the church – even cleaners, workmen and the postman! As this strategy uses personal contacts, produce tickets, even if the event is free, as this helps guests to feel more assured that their presence is expected.

On the night, you will need to consider whether to stay outside for the talk or whether to invite people inside, maybe for food. If you stay outside be aware that people will only have a short attention span due to the cold, so get the talk underway early. If you choose to bring people inside for the talk, do not serve food throughout the display – make it clear on the publicity that food will be served after or during a break in the display. Once people have come inside and are either seated and eating or queuing, give the short talk. Be aware that people will be buying food and may continue talking quietly and that there will be a large proportion of children; this is not the type of event where silence and full concentration can or should be expected. Make the talk short, fun and lively, and people will listen.

Hosting a fireworks display to which the general public will be invited involves specific responsibilities. The website www.fireworksafety.co.uk has a lot of helpful information and also has links to the relevant pages of the DTI website, which gives very detailed information and advice about hosting a public fireworks display.

Fireworks advice in addition to the Fireworks Code

Ensure that fireworks are of the appropriate category for your display. There are four categories:

Category 1:   For use in extremely restricted areas
Indoor fireworks

Category 2:   For use in limited areas, minimum 5
Garden fireworks   metre viewing distance

Category 3:   For use in open areas, e.g. school
Display fireworks   playing fields, minimum 25 metre
                         viewing distance

Category 4:   For use by professionals only

- One person, clearly identified, should be responsible for the fireworks
- Plan the fireworks display carefully and ensure that you have the appropriate aids to launch/set up the fireworks
- Wear eye protection and gloves when lighting fireworks and use a torch for reading instructions
- Provide buckets of water or sand in which to place used sparklers and clearly mark them
- Appoint a first-aider and make sure they are clued-up on burns

Bonfire advice

- Safety organizations generally caution against having a bonfire
- One person, clearly identified, should be responsible for the bonfire
- Bonfires should be at least 18 metres (60 feet) away from houses, trees, hedges, fences or sheds
- Never use petrol, paraffin or other flammable liquids on the bonfire – use domestic fire lighters
- Don't burn anything dangerous (e.g. aerosols) or anything that might give off poisonous fumes (e.g. foam)
- Thoroughly check the bonfire for animals (or children!) before lighting it
- Keep a bucket of water or appropriate fire extinguisher, a fire blanket and a first aid kit handy

41. Recipes

Make your 5th November event more enjoyable and memorable by serving seasonal food. This could be provided free or a small charge could be made – people are used to buying food at secular fireworks displays. There are regional variations on bonfire night menus, so why not serve something different this year? In the north of England revellers eat hot pork pie and mushy peas with mint sauce, followed by parkin (a sticky ginger cake with oatmeal). In the south the tendency is to eat sausages, baked beans and jacket potatoes and toasted marshmallows, as these are associated with cooking on a campfire. And of course toffee apples and bonfire toffee.

Parkin

NB: Parkin is supposed to be left to rest in an airtight container for one week prior to cutting and eating.

12 oz (350 g) medium oatmeal
4 oz (125 g) wholemeal flour
4 oz (125 g) butter
4 oz (125 g) golden syrup
4 oz (125 g) treacle
1 tsp ground ginger
4 tbsp milk
½ tsp bicarbonate of soda

1. Grease an 11 inch (28 cm) × 7 inch (18 cm) cake tin.
2. Pre-heat oven to 325°F (Gas Mark 3, 160°C).

3. Blend together the flour, oats and ginger in a mixing bowl.
4. Gently melt the butter, treacle and golden syrup together in a saucepan (do not boil).
5. Add to the flour, oats and ginger and mix well.
6. Gently heat the milk until lukewarm and stir in the bicarbonate of soda.
7. Add to the oatmeal mixture and beat well.
8. Pour the mixture into the prepared cake tin.
9. Bake in the pre-heated oven for $1\frac{1}{2}$ hours (refer to manufacturer's recommendations if using a fan-assisted oven).
10. Turn out of the tin when cold.

Bonfire toffee

1 lb (450 g) demerara sugar
$\frac{1}{4}$ pint (150 ml) water
3 oz (75 g) butter
8 oz (225 g) golden syrup

1. Lightly oil a 7 inch (18 cm) shallow square tin.
2. Put the water and sugar into a heavy-based pan and stir over a gentle heat until all the sugar has dissolved.
3. Add the remaining ingredients and bring the mixture to the boil. Brush the inside of the pan with cold water just over the level of the toffee mixture to prevent the toffee from boiling over.
4. Boil without stirring, until soft crack stage (270°F on a sweet thermometer or until syrup forms into hard but not brittle threads when dropped into cold water).
5. Carefully pour the mixture into the prepared tin and leave to set.
6. When cooled and properly set, bang the tin hard a few times upside down on a chopping board – the toffee

should crack and fall out of the tin. Don't worry about the irregular shapes and sizes as bonfire toffee is supposed to have a 'home made' look to it.

Toffee apples

8 eating apples
8 lollipop sticks
1 lb (450 g) granulated sugar
2 tbsp clear honey
$\frac{1}{4}$ pint (125 ml) water

1. Wash the apples, remove the stalks and firmly push the sticks into the cores.
2. Put the water, sugar and honey into a heavy-based pan and stir over a gentle heat until all the sugar has dissolved.
3. Bring the mixture to the boil and then boil briskly without stirring until hard crack stage (310°F on a sweet thermometer or until syrup separates into hard and brittle threads when dropped into cold water).
4. Dip each apple into the boiling toffee until it is coated and then leave them to set standing on a greased tin.

Remembrance Sunday

Introduction

Remembrance Sunday is observed on the second Sunday in November, the Sunday nearest to 11th November (the day when the Armistice was signed at the end of World War One).

42. Talk: 'A Day to Remember'

Opening illustration

Have you ever found yourself forgetting what you need to remember and remembering what you need to forget? Ask members of the audience what is the worst thing they have ever forgotten.

At this time of year we remember something very important.

Point 1 (sin and forgiveness): A day for remembering

Today we spend time remembering those who have given their lives for us. (Spend some time talking about those who have given their lives in the past. Mention any wars that are being fought currently.) It is good to be grateful for people who have fought for our freedom. We remember all those lives that were given in the wars of the last two centuries that still affect us today. But let us also remember the life of one person that affected everyone who has ever lived and ever will live, for all time.

(Bible verse: Romans 5:19) Through the obedience of the one man the many will be made righteous.

The death of Jesus made it possible for all to be forgiven.

Point 2 (sin and forgiveness): A day for forgetting

This is a day for remembering, but it's also a day for forgetting. Most of us tend to remember the bad things that people have done to us.

Wouldn't it be amazing if all the bad things you ever did were suddenly forgotten and nobody ever remembered them? You would never be embarrassed when talking to someone you had upset.

Most of us forget what we should remember and remember what we should forget. God chose to forget all our sins, the bad things we do against him.

(Bible verse: Hebrews 8:12) For I will forgive their wickedness and will remember their sins so more.

Today we remember the many lives that were given for people's freedom. It is right that we do this, but let us not forget the one life that was given for the whole world's freedom. Instead of God punishing us for our wrong he gave the life of his own Son Jesus so that we could be forgiven. If we believe in what Jesus did for us, our wrong can be forgiven and forgotten.

Point 3 (response): A day for you to remember

As you look back at today, may it be a day that you remember for the rest of your life. May it be the day you discovered that God chooses not to remember your wrong.

(Bible verse: 2 Corinthians 6:2) Now is the day of salvation.

Now is the time to accept God's offer of life and forgiveness.

• **Admit** to God and yourself that you have sinned; that you have left God out of your life and gone your own way.

- **B**elieve that Jesus came to this world to die on the cross to take your punishment so that you could be forgiven.
- **C**ommit your whole life to God. Turn away from living life your way and start living it God's way.

Do this and mean it, and God will forgive you.

43. Remembrance Sunday Service

If you do not usually observe Remembrance Sunday in your church and have decided to hold a service as an outreach to the older community, ensure that you have briefed your congregation in advance. Remember that although a modern and interactive approach to this service may appeal to a younger audience, the more elderly attendees may be expecting a formal, traditional and 'respectful' approach. Fundamentally Remembrance Sunday is held to remember the dead who fought in the two world wars and other armed conflicts. However, it is also a good time to reflect, offering prayers for peace and wartorn places on earth. Two minutes' silence should be observed at 11 am.

If you don't normally serve refreshments after your service, try adopting this practice, especially after guest services. A chat over a cup of tea and biscuits after the service can make guests feel welcome and give them the chance to experience the friendliness of your church, as well as providing church members with opportunities to invite the guests to other events. Have a team of people on hand to chat to guests, especially if your church is not used to new faces, and have invitations ready for forthcoming church events and regular meetings such as a midweek luncheon club.

It would be a good idea to offer an escort or a lift to elderly guests who might otherwise not be able to attend. This also provides a good opportunity to get to know the guests and to offer friendship and support.

If your resources will stretch to it, hold a special Sunday lunch after the service. The meal should be a traditional affair due to the type of guest expected.

Christmas

Introduction

Never underestimate the evangelistic potential of Christmas. Many people who would not usually come to church are willing (if not wanting!) to cross the threshold at this time of year. Don't waste the opportunity!

This section includes a wide variety of suggested events to host over the Christmas period: a Christmas meal, a Christmas play, a Christmas puppet show and various carol services. Try to think strategically: a well-targeted carol service and a well-advertised Christmas play may establish new contacts in the community.

Always think ahead to the next event; if new contacts do visit your church over the Christmas period, ensure that you have thought about how to help them feel they are welcome to come again. Ensure that the next event is advertised and that invitations are available. Also ensure that details of weekly services and clubs are well advertised.

44. Talk: 'The Problem with Christmas'

Opening illustration

One little boy's illusions were shattered when he was hit in the face as he tried to unmask a supermarket Santa. Christopher Chantler, aged eight, was amazed to find Father Christmas sitting in his grotto in a supermarket store when he had just seen him in another shop a mile away. Anxious not to be seen as an impostor, Santa said that he had flown to the Rochdale store, arriving ahead of the boy, who had travelled by car. Christopher remained suspicious and gave Santa's white whiskers a tug to check their authenticity. Father Christmas sought to protect his identity, but in the process caught the boy across the face, reducing him to tears. His mother claimed the blow was deliberate. Santa and the supermarket claimed that it was an accident and said they were deeply sorry. Either way, Santa will never be the same again to Christopher. His mother commented, 'He said that he doesn't want Father Christmas to come to our house any more because he does nasty things. He was absolutely heart-broken.'

Christmas can often be a let down.

Christmas can often be a problem.

The problem with Christmas is when it's over . . .

Point 1 (sin): Overindulging

There are 180 calories in an average mince pie. It takes forty-five minutes of continual hoovering to burn them off. In

199

1650 mince pies were considered to be indulgent and far too rich, so an Act of Parliament was passed authorizing the imprisonment of anyone found guilty of eating a mince pie.

We all know that feeling of having eaten more than our body can take. 'Never again' are the immortal words. That is until next Christmas. Then the same thing happens again! We overindulge and worry about taking it off in the New Year. Jesus said in the Bible:

(Bible verse: John 10:10) I have come that they may have life, and have it to the full.

We overindulge in all areas of our life, trying to find fulfilment. We do and say and think things that hurt us, hurt others and reject God. We say, 'I want to live my life my way and I don't care about the repercussions.' The Bible calls this 'sin'.

Christmas is about Jesus coming to earth to die on a cross and take the punishment for this sin. Because of what started at the first Christmas, we can be forgiven, know God personally and find fulfilment as a result.

And there are no bad repercussions later – only blessings in heaven!

Point 2 (the cross): Overspending

We spend money on presents in order to express love towards people. God spent and gave what was necessary and expressed his love for us. Our forgiveness cost him his own Son Jesus.

(Bible verse: John 3:16) For God so loved the world that he gave his one and only Son, that whoever believes in him shall not perish but have eternal life.

Point 3 (response): Over too quickly

We certainly cannot improve on what happened that first Christmas, but we can improve on the way we celebrate it today. Christmas does not last very long and yet what happened on that first Christmas was, and is, long lasting.

Christmas was, and is, all about God having a lasting effect on our lives.

* Admit that you have left God out of Christmas because you have left him out of your life.
* Believe that Jesus came into this world that first Christmas to die on the cross to take your punishment so that you could be forgiven.
* Commit your life to God now and for ever. Turn away from living life your way and start living it God's way.

Do this and mean it, and let God change your life for ever this Christmas.

45. Christmas Meal

Holding a Christmas meal is a good way to involve guests with your church in a non-threatening way. Those who don't go out to work (single parents, the elderly, the unemployed) are unlikely to be invited to a Christmas 'do', so it's a great opportunity to fill the gap with a low-key taster event. It is common practice to invite an after-dinner speaker to make a short and interesting address at dinner events, and this provides an opportunity to briefly share the real message of Christmas and talk about the activities your church is holding over the festive season. The talk should be given during the after-dinner coffee, but it is important to ensure that the waiting/catering team are not clearing tables, noisily washing up or talking loudly during the gospel message!

If your church has the facilities and resources (catering team, hall, well-equipped kitchen, tables, crockery and cutlery) then you could hold the meal 'in house'. However, other options include hiring a local function room and either using their kitchen or getting them to cater for you. It is sensible to charge for the event, not only to help cover the price of the food, but also so that you are able to inform the caterers of the number of guests that will be attending. The church may decide to adopt a concessions policy or ask that people buy tickets for their non-Christian friends if necessary.

Think carefully about the type and number of guests you are likely to attract. Unless you are planning an event for a small number of adventurous guests it is best to stick to a traditional menu that will appeal to all tastes and not disappoint. The following menu suggestion (although a bit boring) is a safe bet.

STARTER

Cream of Tomato Soup

MAIN COURSE

Roast Turkey with Stuffing
Roast Potatoes
Carrots
Brussel Sprouts
Gravy

DESSERT

Christmas Pudding and Custard
or
Trifle

Coffee and After Dinner Mints

Take time to decorate the room and tables in a festive manner; tablecloths and decorations make all the difference! Try alternating green and red paper tablecloths, and collect some pine cones, spray them silver and gold and arrange them with some evergreen and tinsel to make table centrepieces. You could even get the Sunday school to make candleholders (see Idea 46) for the event, and these could be given as Christmas gifts to guests at the end of the evening. Make Christian Christmas crackers (see Idea 46). Display the menu on each table. Have Christmas music playing as guests enter, although not too loud as the event aims to encourage friendly conversation with those from outside the church.

Ensure that you have a well-presented programme of your Christmas services and events at each place setting. This could also include a short paragraph about your church and the regular activities it provides. Maybe give a Christmas card and Christmas tract to each guest (Christmas tracts and festive 'audio tracts' on CD are available from The Goings Trust, PO Box 350, Huddersfield HD2 2YB or by email at goingstrust@ntlworld.com).

46. Christmas Craft

Christian crackers

Make your own Christmas crackers using tissue paper and loo rolls. Each cracker should contain a Bible verse instead of a joke. Put in a 'halo' of tinsel for people to wear instead of a hat, and a small colourful wrapped sweet. You can buy cracker snaps from most joke/toy shops; alternatively you could ask people to make their own bang noises when they pull the crackers!

Christmas candle-holders

Make candle-holders using large Christmas biscuit cutters and salt dough (see recipe and diagrams following). You could add decoration to the basic shape using extra salt dough (e.g. baubles and garlands on Christmas tree shapes, berries on holly, nose on Rudolf). Once baked, finish off the candle-holders with a coat of clear varnish.

If the candle-holders are to be made by children and given as gifts, attach a sticky label to the back of each finished candle-holder with a Christmas message from the child who made it (e.g. 'Happy Christmas from Amy, aged 8').

Salt dough recipe

200 ml water
300 g plain flour
300 g salt
1 tbsp vegetable oil

Mix all the ingredients together until smooth, or blend in a food mixer. Model as below, then slow bake on a low heat until completely dry.

1. Use Christmas themed biscuit cutters to cut a 20 mm thick biscuit of salt dough.
2. Use an empty tealight case to cut a circle from the centre of the biscuit.
3. Cut a matching shape biscuit 5 mm thick. Moisten the biscuit with water and attach to the back of the biscuit with the hole to provide a base for the tea light.
4. Paint and decorate if required before baking.

47. Talk: 'A Christmas Carol'

Ebeneezer Scrooge was haunted in three ways.

Point 1 (sin): Haunted by the past

It is possible to be haunted by the past. Buster Edwards, the great train robber, gave himself up because he could not stand the guilt of what he had done. It is amazing too how even seemingly small things we have done can haunt us.

A Christmas carol called 'On Christmas night all Christians sing' has these words:

> Then why should men on earth be sad,
> Since our redeemer [has] made us glad,
> When from our sin he set us free,
> All to gain our liberty?

(Bible verse: Matthew 1:21) You are to give him the name Jesus, because he will save his people from their sins.

Jesus came to forgive the sins we have committed, whether large or small. The only way to deal with the past is to let God erase it.

Point 2 (cross): Haunted by the present

It is possible to be haunted by the present. We live in a world where there is not much security. Our circumstances can change so easily. Since the destruction of the twin towers on

11th September 2001, we have been made acutely aware of how easily things can change.

The Christmas carol 'O Little Town of Bethlehem' says:

O Holy Child of Bethlehem descend to us we pray,
Cast out our sin and enter in, be born in us today.

(Bible verse: 1 Peter 5:7) Cast all your anxiety on him because he cares for you.

Jesus showed how he cared for us by dying on the cross. He wants to be born in you today. This takes place when we believe Jesus died on the cross for us, taking the punishment for our wrong. When Jesus comes in, he enables us to live in peace with God now.

Point 3 (response): Haunted by the future

It is possible to be haunted by the future. It is estimated that six out of ten men, seven out of ten women and 50 per cent of young people read their stars. We want to know what the future holds.

Another Christmas carol says:

Good Christian men rejoice,
With heart and soul and voice,
Now ye need not fear the grave,
Peace, Peace . . .

God brings peace even into the thing that is most frightening in the future: death.

(Bible verse: Jeremiah 29:11) 'For I know the plans I have for you,' declares the Lord, 'plans to prosper you and not to harm you, plans to give you hope and a future.'

We need not fear the future because God has a plan for our lives. By following God's plan for our lives, only that which God allows to happen to us will happen. Do not think about getting to know what the future holds. It is better to know who holds the future.

- Admit to God and yourself that you have sinned; that you have left God out of your life and gone your own way.
- Believe that Jesus came to this world to die on the cross to take your punishment so that you could be forgiven.
- Commit your whole life to God. Turn away from living life your way and start living it God's way.

By doing this and meaning it, you can be set free from the past, live in peace now and have hope for the future.

48. Christmas Presentation: 'Scrooge'

Put on a presentation based upon Charles Dickens' *A Christmas Carol*. The adaptation provided here lasts approximately forty minutes and can be followed immediately by the talk detailed in Idea 47, making a programme length of around one hour and fifteen minutes.

Christmas carols could be sung before or after the presentation if desired, and mince pies and mulled wine or non-alcoholic punch could be served afterwards, providing an opportunity to talk to visitors in a relaxed environment.

Possible arrangements

The play will work just as well with a minimal cast (e.g. five) as with a full twenty-five member cast. However, awareness of the tightness of timing between changes is essential and a number of dress rehearsals may have to be held. It is important to ensure that each actor playing several parts has a distinguishable identity, so clever costuming is vital. The ghosts are all easily identifiable, but Fezziwig, Bob Cratchit and Old Joe, as well as Mrs Cratchit, Mrs Smithers, Mrs Dilber and Caroline, and any children playing different roles, all need to be clearly discernible. I suggest using cheap wigs (approximately £10 each from joke shops), fake facial hair for the men (combinations of moustaches, sideburns, beards, eyebrows) and hats, as well as completely different costumes and colour schemes. The actors should adopt different accents and body posture if it is within their capability.

Arrangement for five:

MALE 1:   Scrooge

MALE 2:   Charity collector (off stage), young Scrooge, errand boy (off stage), Ghost of Christmas Future

MALE 3:   Marley's Ghost (off stage), Fezziwig, Bob Cratchit, banker 2 (off stage), Old Joe

FEMALE 1:   Ghost of Christmas Past, Mrs Cratchit, banker 1 (off stage), Mrs Smithers

FEMALE 2:   Young woman, Ghost of Christmas Present, Mrs Dilber, Caroline

Arrangement for eight:

MALE 1:   Scrooge

MALE 2:   Charity collector (off stage), young Scrooge, banker 1 (off stage)

MALE 3:   Marley's Ghost (off stage), Bob Cratchit, banker 2 (off stage)

MALE 4:   Fezziwig, Ghost of Christmas Future

FEMALE 1:   Ghost of Christmas Past, Mrs Cratchit, Mrs Smithers

FEMALE 2:   Young woman, Mrs Dilber, Caroline

FEMALE 3:   Ghost of Christmas Present, Old Joe

MALE CHILD: Scrooge as child, errand boy, Tiny Tim

Suggested rehearsal timetable

Preparation and rehearsals for the event should start in September for a production due mid-December. It is a good idea to schedule weekly rehearsals of approximately one-and-a-half hours' duration over a period of twelve weeks or so, culminating in the final week with a dress rehearsal and the performances.

Rehearsal	Activity
1	Full cast read through
2	Scene 1 – Scrooge, Ghost of Christmas Past, Fezziwig
3	Scene 1 – Young Scrooge, young woman
4	Scene 2 – Scrooge, Ghost of Christmas Present
5	Scene 2 – Bob and Mrs Cratchit
6	Scene 3 – Scrooge and Ghost of Christmas Future
7	Scene 3 – Old Joe, Mrs Smithers, Mrs Dilber
8	Scene 3 – Bob and Mrs Cratchit
9	Scene 1 (All lines learned by this time)
10	Scene 2
11	Scene 3
12	Full run through
13	Dress rehearsal

Costuming

The following provides suggestions for simple costuming for the characters. All the costumes can be produced using only four dress patterns:

- Ghost costume: hooded choir gowns in white, green and black (Simplicity pattern 9887)
- Female costume: simple high-waisted, long-sleeved, ankle-length dress in different colours (Simplicity pattern 8191)
- Male costume: waistcoat and cravat in varying colours (Simplicity pattern 8808), accompanied by shirt and trousers
- Scrooge nightdress (Simplicity pattern 9898)

Cast

CHARITY COLLECTOR:	Male or female, off-stage voice
SCROOGE:	Male, elderly
MARLEY'S GHOST:	Male, off-stage voice
GHOST OF CHRISTMAS PAST:	Male or female
SCROOGE AS A CHILD:	Optional, young boy
FEZZIWIG:	Male, could be off-stage voice
YOUNG SCROOGE:	Male, late teens/early twenties
YOUNG WOMAN:	Female, late teens/early twenties
GHOST OF CHRISTMAS PRESENT:	Male or female
ERRAND BOY:	Male or female child, could be off-stage voice
MRS CRATCHIT:	Female
BOB CRATCHIT:	Male
CRATCHIT CHILDREN:	Optional male or female, could also have a Tiny Tim
GHOST OF CHRISTMAS FUTURE:	Male or female, no speaking, totally cloaked
BANKER 1:	Male, could be off-stage voice (if off stage could be female putting on a gruff voice)
BANKER 2:	Male, could be off-stage voice (if off stage could be female putting on a gruff voice)
MRS DILBER:	Female (could be male by slightly changing the script)
OLD JOE:	Male (could be female by referring to her as Old Josey)
MRS SMITHERS:	Female (could be male by slightly changing the script)
CAROLINE:	Female

Prologue

Blackout throughout the entire prologue. Actors stay off stage and voices are amplified into the auditorium. Scene starts with a short hearty burst of 'God Rest You Merry Gentlemen', followed by silence, then a sound of knocking, and the creak of a door opening.

C. COLLECTOR Scrooge and Marley's, I believe. Have I the pleasure of addressing Mr Scrooge, or Mr Marley?

SCROOGE Mr Marley has been dead these seven years. He died seven years ago, this very night.

C. COLLECTOR We have no doubt his generosity is well represented by his surviving partner. At this festive season of the year, Mr Scrooge, it is more than usually desirable that we should make some slight provision for the poor and destitute, who suffer greatly at the present time. Many thousands are in want of common necessaries; hundreds of thousands are in want of common comforts, sir.

SCROOGE Are there no prisons?

C. COLLECTOR Plenty of prisons.

SCROOGE And the union workhouses? Are they still in operation?

C. COLLECTOR They are, still. I wish I could say they were not.

SCROOGE Oh! I'm very glad to hear it. I was afraid, from what you said at first, that something had occurred to bring them to a halt.

C. COLLECTOR They scarcely provide Christian cheer to body or soul! So a few of us are endeavouring to raise some money to buy the poor some meat and drink and means of warmth.

We choose this time, because it is a time, above all others, when want is keenly felt by many, whilst for the fortunate few, abundance rejoices. What shall I put you down for?

SCROOGE Nothing!

C. COLLECTOR You wish to be anonymous?

SCROOGE I wish to be left alone. I don't make merry myself at Christmas and I can't afford to make idle people merry. I help to support the establishments I have mentioned – they cost enough; and those who are badly off must go there.

C. COLLECTOR Many can't go there, and many would rather die.

SCROOGE If they would rather die, then let them and decrease the surplus population. Good afternoon!

An ethereal strain of 'God Rest You Merry Gentlemen' followed by silence. Then the sound of whistling wind and a banging door.

MARLEY'S GHOST You will be haunted by three spirits. Expect the first tomorrow, when the bell tolls twelve. Expect the second on the next night at the same hour. The third upon the next night when the last stroke of twelve has ceased to ring.

Scene 1

Dim lights come up on Scrooge asleep in a chair in his room. A clock rings the four quarters and then chimes twelve. After the twelfth chime has rung, a whistling wind is heard and the ghost enters in the semi-darkness, holding a candle or lantern. The ghost stands for a while watching Scrooge, until he is woken by the chill that has entered the room.

SCROOGE	Are you the spirit whose coming was fore-told to me?
C. PAST	I am.
SCROOGE	Who and what are you?
C. PAST	I am the Ghost of Christmas Past.
SCROOGE	Long past?
C. PAST	No. Your past.
SCROOGE	What business brings you here?
C. PAST	Your welfare.
SCROOGE	Well, I'm much obliged but surely a night of unbroken rest would have been more condu-cive to that end.
C. PAST	Your reclamation, then. Take heed. Rise. And walk with me.

The ghost makes to leave, but Scrooge rises from his chair to stop it.

SCROOGE	Wait! I cannot pass through the window as you. I am mortal, and liable to fall.
C. PAST	Bear but a touch of my hand, and you shall be upheld.

The ghost touches Scrooge and he finds he is able to move alongside the ghost out of the window. A change in lighting shows that they are now looking at a daylight scene.

SCROOGE	Where are we? What's that? Wait. Look. Good heaven! I was bred in this place. I was a boy here.
C. PAST	You recollect the way?

SCROOGE   Remember it! I could walk it blindfold.

C. PAST   Strange then to have forgotten it for so many
                 years. Let us go on.

There is a sound of children playing, shouting, laughing.
Scrooge watches the scene that takes place off the stage as if
behind the audience.

SCROOGE   Why, it's Farmer Barton and his old cart!
                 Look at Bess the cart horse; how I used to
                 wish I could jump up on her for a ride! And
                 see the others following behind in the gigs
                 and on ponies – they're heading for the
                 river, what a row they're making! They
                 made the river trip every Christmas Eve; all
                 the children from the village went down to
                 the water, frozen hard as iron most years. It
                 was where Fan caught her chill the year
                 she . . .

C. PAST   Fan was your sister?

SCROOGE   Yes, Fan was my sister. Oh, look, there she is
                 now! Fan! Fan . . .

C. PAST   These are but shadows of the things that
                 have been. They have no consciousness of us.

SCROOGE   Oh Fan, oh Fan.

The sounds of the children fade and the lighting changes again
and is directed towards stage right, where a young boy sits at
a desk doing schoolwork. This action could also be 'imaginary'
if a young boy actor is not available.

C. PAST   We approach an empty school yard. But no,
                 look, the school is not quite deserted. A soli-
                 tary child, neglected by his friends, is left
                 there still.

SCROOGE	Do you think I don't remember?
C. PAST	You had forgotten.
SCROOGE	Not forgotten, just not remembered. Poor boy. I wish . . . ah, but it's too late now.
C. PAST	What is the matter?
SCROOGE	Nothing. Nothing. There was a boy singing a Christmas carol at my door last night. I should like to have given him something, that's all.

The lights change and are directed to stage left. The boy leaves, taking his desk and props with him, but leaving the chair.

C. PAST	Let us see another Christmas. Do you recognize this door?
SCROOGE	Know it! I was apprenticed here! Why, it's old Fezziwig! Bless his heart; it's Fezziwig alive again.

Enter Fezziwig stage left. He addresses an imaginary young Scrooge and his friend Dick.

FEZZIWIG	Yo ho, there! Ebenezer! Dick!
SCROOGE	And Dick Wilkins, to be sure. Bless me, yes. There he is. He was very much attached to me was Dick, my fellow apprentice. Dick! Dear Dick.
FEZZIWIG	Yo ho, my boys! No more work tonight. Christmas Eve, Dick! Christmas, Ebenezer! Let's have the shutters up before a man can say Jack Robinson. Clear away, my lads, and let's have lots of room here. Hurry up, Dick! Come on, Ebenezer.

Cheerful knocking is heard off stage.

> Open up, Dick, that'll be the fiddler. Ebenezer – round the back and help Mrs Fezziwig with her baskets – come on, lad, or the pies will go cold. Hey ho, the dancers will be here at six, boys, and we'll dance past midnight if I have my way!

Fezziwig leaves the stage with a little jig.

C. PAST	A small matter, to make these silly folks so full of gratitude.
SCROOGE	Small!
C. PAST	Why! Is it not? He has spent but a few pounds of your mortal money, three or four perhaps. Is that so much that he deserves this praise?
SCROOGE	It isn't that. It isn't that, Spirit. He had the power to render us happy or unhappy; to make our work light or burdensome; a pleasure or a toil. A quick word of praise here, an appreciative look there, things so slight and insignificant that they are impossible to recount. The happiness he gave us in this way was as great as if it cost a fortune.

Scrooge feels the spirit's glance, and stops.

C. PAST	What is the matter?
SCROOGE	Nothing in particular.
C. PAST	Something, I think.
SCROOGE	No. No. I should like to be able to say a word or two to my clerk just now. That's all.

The spirit looks at the candle it is carrying.

C. PAST   My time grows short. Quick! We must see
                 one shadow more.

*The lights change and are directed stage right. Enter Scrooge
as a young man with an attractive young woman. Young
woman takes a seat and turns from the young Scrooge.*

YOUNG WOMAN   It matters little to you, very little. I am no
                 longer the desire of your heart; you focus
                 your affections and your time upon
                 another. I only hope that it can cheer and
                 comfort you as you grow old, as I would
                 have tried to do.
YOUNG SCROOGE   What other lover do I have?
YOUNG WOMAN   A golden one.
YOUNG SCROOGE   Oh, can I never do right? On the one hand
                 we must be seen to despise poverty as a
                 vile plague on the human race, whilst with
                 the other we crush those that through
                 hard work pursue the security and
                 comfort that wealth brings. Such is the
                 way of this fickle world!
YOUNG WOMAN   You desire that security and comfort too
                 much. The dreams and aspirations you
                 had when we first met have all now fallen
                 by the wayside, victims of your now all
                 engrossing passion: gain.
YOUNG SCROOGE   What then? Even if I have grown so much
                 wiser, what then? I am not changed
                 towards you. Am I?

The young woman shakes her head.

YOUNG WOMAN   Our betrothal was agreed many years
                 past. It was made when we were both poor

	and content to be so, until, in good season, we could improve our worldly fortune by our hard work. You are changed. When it was made, you were another man.
YOUNG SCROOGE	I was a boy.
YOUNG WOMAN	You know that you are not what you were. I am. Our union which promised happiness when we shared a dream, is fraught with misery now that you have set yourself upon a different path. How often I have thought of this, I will not say. It is enough that I have thought of it, and release you from your promise.
YOUNG SCROOGE	Have I ever sought release?
YOUNG WOMAN	In words? No, never.
YOUNG SCROOGE	In what, then?
YOUNG WOMAN	In your changed nature, in your altered spirit, in your striding ahead down a new and unmerciful path. Ebenezer! If we were not betrothed, tell me, would you seek me out and try to win me now? Ah, no.
YOUNG SCROOGE	You think not?
YOUNG WOMAN	I would gladly think otherwise if I could. Heaven knows. When I have learned a truth like this, how hard it is to accept it! Yet I do; and I release you. With a full heart, for the love of him you once were.

Young Scrooge is about to speak, but the young woman has her head turned from him and resumes.

YOUNG WOMAN	You may have pain in this – the memory of what is past half-makes me hope you

will have. But in a very brief time you will dismiss the memory, gladly, as an unprofitable dream from which you happily awoke. May you be happy in the life you have chosen.

The young woman rises and leaves the room. The young Scrooge hesitates a while, then looks at his watch and walks swiftly off in the opposite direction.

SCROOGE   Spirit! Show me no more. Conduct me home. Why do you delight to torture me? No more! I don't wish to see it! Show me no more!

C. PAST   I told you these were shadows of the things that have been. That they are what they are, do not blame me.

SCROOGE   Remove me from this place! I cannot bear it. Leave me! Take me back! Haunt me no longer!

Scrooge looks around, desperate for an idea. He sees the ghost's candle. He moves towards the candle; the ghost tries to prevent him. After a brief struggle Scrooge gains the candle and blows it out. At that moment the ghost collapses on the floor and the lights go out.

Scene 2

Scrooge is seated in the chair in his room, awake this time as the clock chimes twelve. After the final stroke the faint strains of 'God Rest You Merry, Gentlemen' can be heard as if from the next room, and a warm yellow glow issues forth from off stage. The music gets louder, but still nothing happens. The clock ticks loudly.

SCROOGE

I had prepared myself for much. I was ready for a good broad field of strange appearances, and nothing between a baby or a rhinoceros would have astonished me much. But this! I, being prepared for almost anything, am not prepared, by any means, for nothing! No one, nothing comes. Yet something happens and this glow that has streamed across the floor since the clock proclaimed the hour is more alarming than a dozen ghosts. It appears to have its source from the adjoining room.

Ah, if it will not approach me, I must seek it.

Scrooge rises and makes his way to the door of the adjoining room. As soon as he approaches, the ghost speaks.

C. PRESENT

Come in! Come in, and know me better, man!

Scrooge leaves stage and then comes back with the ghost. The ghost has an arm around Scrooge's shoulders in a familiar fashion and is leading him back on stage.

C. PRESENT

I am the Ghost of Christmas Present. Look upon me. You have never seen the like of me before!

SCROOGE

Never! Spirit, conduct me where you will. I went forth last night on compulsion, and I learnt a lesson which is working now. Tonight, if you have anything to teach me, let me profit by it.

C. PRESENT

Touch my sleeve.

Change of light. An errand boy runs across the street.

ERRAND BOY	Merry Christmas! A merry Christmas to all!
SCROOGE	Why have you brought me here? I know nothing of this poor neighbourhood.

Mrs Cratchit enters stage right and stands (in her kitchen) staring off stage. As Scrooge looks inside, the lights focus more upon the Cratchit dwelling.

C. PRESENT	Look inside, Ebenezer. Look inside.
SCROOGE	Still I know them not.
C. PRESENT	Turn then and look down the street at him who approaches.
SCROOGE	I see, Spirit, it is Bob Cratchit, my clerk. Is this his poor dwelling?
C. PRESENT	You guess aright.

Bob Cratchit joins his wife on stage.

MRS CRATCHIT	And how did little Tim behave?
BOB CRATCHIT	As good as gold, and better. Somehow he gets thoughtful sitting by himself so much, and thinks the strangest things you ever heard. He told me, coming home, that he hoped the people saw him in the church, because he was a cripple and it might be pleasant to them to remember upon Christmas Day who made lame beggars walk and blind men see! Tiny Tim is growing strong and hearty in spirit, if not in body, Mrs Cratchit.

Lights fade on Cratchit dwelling.

SCROOGE	Spirit, tell me, who is Tiny Tim?

C. PRESENT	He is Cratchit's boy. He has been crippled since birth and grows weaker each month.
SCROOGE	Spirit! Tell me if Tiny Tim will live.
C. PRESENT	I see a vacant seat in the poor chimney corner, and a crutch without an owner, carefully preserved. If these shadows remain unaltered by the future, the child will die.
SCROOGE	No, no! Oh no, kind Spirit! Say he will be spared.
C. PRESENT	If these shadows remain unaltered by the future, the child will die! But what then? If he be likely to die, he had better do it, and decrease the surplus population.

Scrooge hangs his head to hear his own words quoted by the spirit, and is overcome with penitence and grief.

C. PRESENT	Man, if man you be in heart, hold back your wicked conceit until you have discovered what the surplus is, and where it is. Will you decide what men shall live, what men shall die? It may be, that in the sight of heaven, you are more worthless and less fit to live than millions like this poor man's child.

Scrooge bows his head. Lights raise back to Cratchit dwelling. Scrooge looks up when Bob Cratchit holds a glass and toasts:

BOB CRATCHIT	Mr Scrooge! I'll give you Mr Scrooge, the Founder of the Feast!
MRS CRATCHIT	The Founder of the Feast indeed! I wish I had him here. I'd give him a piece of my mind to feast upon, and I hope he'd have a good appetite for it.
BOB CRATCHIT	My dear. The children. Christmas Day.

MRS CRATCHIT   It should be Christmas Day, I am sure, on which one drinks the health of such an odious, stingy, hard, unfeeling man as Mr Scrooge. You know he is, Robert. Nobody knows it better than you do, poor fellow.

BOB CRATCHIT   My dear, Christmas Day.

MRS CRATCHIT   I'll drink his health for your sake and the day's, not for his. Long life to him. A merry Christmas and a happy New Year! He'll be very merry and very happy, I have no doubt!

Blackout while all characters exit except Scrooge.

Scene 3

During the blackout the clock chimes twelve. The lights come back on and Scrooge has not moved from his previous position, yet the Ghost of Christmas Present has disappeared and the Ghost of Christmas Future stands behind Scrooge, as yet unseen by him.

SCROOGE   Twelve? Has my last encounter lasted a full day and night?

Scrooge turns, sees the ghost and trembles.

SCROOGE   Am I in the presence of the Ghost of Christmas Yet To Come?

The spirit says nothing, but points forward with its hand.

SCROOGE   You are about to show me shadows of the things that have not happened, but will happen in the time before us. Is that so, Spirit?

The spirit gives no reply.

SCROOGE   Ghost of the Future! I fear you more than any spectre I have seen. But as I know your purpose is to do me good, and as I hope to live to be another man from what I was, I am prepared to bear you company, and do it with a thankful heart. Will you not speak to me?

It gives him no reply. The hand continues to point straight before them.

SCROOGE   Lead on. Lead on. The night is waning fast, and it is precious time to me, I know. Lead on, Spirit.

Two of Scrooge's business acquaintances enter stage left. (Alternatively, the following conversation can be heard off stage.)

BANKER 1   I don't know much about it either way. I only know he's dead.

BANKER 2   When did he die?

BANKER 1   Last night, I believe.

BANKER 2   What was the matter with him? I thought he'd never die.

BANKER 1   Goodness knows!

BANKER 2   What has he done with his money?

BANKER 1   I haven't heard. Left it to his company, perhaps. He hasn't left it to me, that's all I know! *(They laugh.)* It's likely to be a very cheap funeral, for upon my life I don't know of anybody to go to it.

BANKER 2   Suppose we volunteer? I don't mind going if

a lunch is provided. But I must be fed if I make the effort. *(They laugh again.)*

BANKER 1   Well, I never wear black gloves, and I never eat lunch. But I'll offer to go, if you will. When I come to think of it, I'm not at all sure that I wasn't his most particular friend; for we used to stop and speak whenever we met. Bye, bye.

Bankers leave stage.

SCROOGE   I know them both! Business colleagues! Who can they be conversing about in such a terrible way? Have they no respect for a dead man?

A change of light to a murky terrible neighbourhood. A grubby, tatty man enters. Two shady-looking women enter from opposite sides of the stage and move towards the man.

MRS DILBER   I got business with you first, Joe. Alone! You can see her after we're done.

OLD JOE   Tsk, tsk! Come into the parlour, Mrs Dilber. You too, Mrs Smithers; you ain't a stranger.

Mrs Smithers starts to get things out of her bundle.

OLD JOE   Stop till I shut the door of the shop. Ahhh. How it creaks, just like me old bones, just like me old bones! Ha, ha! Come into the parlour. Come into the parlour. Both of you. Don't hold back. We're well matched – we all share the same calling. There's nothing to be ashamed of.

MRS SMITHERS   Don't fret yourself, Mrs Dilber. Every

	person has a right to take care of themselves. He always did.
MRS DILBER	That's true, indeed. No man more so.
MRS SMITHERS	Why then, don't stand staring as if you was afraid, woman! Who's the wiser? We're not going to pick holes in each other's coats, I suppose?
MRS DILBER/ OLD JOE	No, indeed!
MRS DILBER	We should hope not!
MRS SMITHERS	Very well, then! That's enough. Who's the worse for the loss of a few things like these? Not a dead man, I suppose.
MRS DILBER	No, indeed!
MRS SMITHERS	If he wanted to keep them after he was dead, why wasn't he more natural in his lifetime? If he had been, he'd have had somebody to look after him when he was struck with death, instead of lying gasping out his last there, alone by himself.
MRS DILBER	It's the truest word that ever was spoke. It's a judgement on him.

Mrs Smithers weighs her sack.

MRS SMITHERS	I wish it was a little *heavier* judgement! And it would have been, you may depend upon it, if I could have laid my hands on anything else! Open up the bundle, Old Joe, and let me know the value of it. Speak out plain. I'm not afraid to be the first, nor afraid for her to see it. Open the bundle, Joe.

Old Joe goes through Mrs Smithers' sack and produces sheets and towels, a few old clothes, two old-fashioned silver teaspoons, a pair of sugar tongs and a few boots. Joe hands over a few pence.

OLD JOE	I always give too much to friends. It's a weakness of mine, and that's the way I ruin myself. That's your account. If you asked me for another penny, I'd repent of being so generous and knock off half a crown.
MRS DILBER	And now undo my bundle, Joe.

Joe drags out a large and heavy roll of some dark material.

OLD JOE	What do you call this? Bed curtains?
MRS DILBER	Aye, bed curtains.
OLD JOE	You don't mean to say you took them down, rings and all, with him lying there?
MRS DILBER	Yes I do, and why not?
OLD JOE	You were born to make your fortune and you'll certainly do it.
MRS DILBER	I certainly shan't hold back my hand, when I can get anything in it by reaching it out, for the sake of such a man as he was, I promise you, Joe. Mind the blankets by the lamp, now.
OLD JOE	His blankets?
MRS DILBER	Whose else's do you think? He isn't likely to take cold without them, I dare say.
OLD JOE	I hope he didn't die of anything catching. Eh?
MRS DILBER	Don't you be afraid of that. I ain't so fond of his company that I'd loiter about him for such things, if he did.

Old Joe is satisfied with that and continues to rummage through the bundle, pulling out a bed shirt and starting to examine it.

MRS DILBER   Ah. You may look through that shirt till your eyes ache; but you won't find a hole in it, nor a threadbare place. It's the best he had, and a fine one too. They'd have wasted it, if it hadn't been for me.

OLD JOE   What do you call wasting of it?

MRS DILBER   Putting it on him to be buried in, to be sure. Somebody was fool enough to do it, but I took it off again.

Scrooge listens to this dialogue in horror.

MRS DILBER   Ha! This is the end of it, you see. He frightened everyone away from him when he was alive, to profit us when he was dead.

The group laugh together and then leave the stage, Old Joe taking both the bundles and their contents with him.

SCROOGE   Spirit! I see, I see. The case of this unhappy man might be my own. My life tends that way now. Merciful heaven! If there is any person in the town who feels emotion caused by this man's death, show that person to me, Spirit, I beseech you.

A young woman appears with a letter and reads out loud.

CAROLINE   Caroline, I have been unable to gain an audience, as I had hoped, with our creditor. It appears that he was not only very ill, but dying. When I left last night, it seemed that we were ruined, but new hope appears. We had hoped beyond hope that a miracle would occur and that he would relent. He is past relenting. He is dead! I know not yet to whom our debt will be transferred, but it must be exceedingly unlikely that we shall find so merciless a creditor again. We will sleep lighter tonight, my love. I return upon the morrow. Your loving husband. Richard.

Young woman exits from the stage.

SCROOGE   No! Not just emotion. Some concern, some kindliness, Spirit, please. Let me see some tenderness connected with a death.

Mrs Cratchit (and family of children if available) enters the stage with a Bible and sits to read in a choked voice.

MRS CRATCHIT   And Jesus called a little child unto him, and set him in the midst of them, and said, 'Verily I say unto you, except ye be converted, and become as little children, ye shall not enter into the kingdom of heaven.'

She stops reading to wipe her tears, and addresses the children sitting at her feet, who are listening to the Bible reading.

MRS CRATCHIT   The reading, it hurts my eyes. See! They're better again now. It makes them weak by candlelight; and I wouldn't show weak eyes to Mr Cratchit when he comes home for the world. It must be near his time. But I think he's walked a little slower than he used, these last few evenings. I have known him walk with . . . I have known him walk with Tiny Tim upon his shoulder, very fast indeed. But he was very light to carry and

his father loved him so, that it was no
trouble – no trouble. Oh! There he is at the
door!

*Bob Cratchit enters the stage and his wife hurries to greet him,
drying her tears. He tries to be cheerful with his wife.*

MRS CRATCHIT   Sunday. You went today, then, Robert?
BOB CRATCHIT   Yes, my dear. I wish you could have gone. It
               would have done you good to see how green
               a place it is. But you'll see it often. I prom-
               ised him that I would walk there on a
               Sunday.

Bob breaks down in distress.

BOB CRATCHIT   My little, little child! My little child!

*Bob Cratchit leaves the stage in emotion. After a pause and a
long distant stare, Mrs Cratchit follows.*

SCROOGE   Spectre, something informs me that our
               parting moment is at hand. I know it, but I
               know not how. Tell me what man that was
               about whom we have heard such little
               regard.
                   This street, through which we hurry now,
               is where my place of occupation is, and has
               been for a length of time. I see the house. Let
               me behold what I shall be, in days to come.

The spirit stops; the hand is pointed elsewhere.

SCROOGE   The house is yonder. Why do you point
               away?

234 50 FESTIVE IDEAS FOR EVANGELISTIC EVENTS

The finger undergoes no change. The backdrop changes to a churchyard scene.

SCROOGE   Before I draw nearer to that stone to which you point, answer me one question. Are these the shadows of the things that *will* be, or are they shadows of things that *may* be, only?

The ghost points downward to a grave close to where they are standing.

SCROOGE   Our deeds have consequences if we persist in certain courses. But if the courses be departed from, the ends will change. Say it is thus with what you show me!

The spirit remains still and silent. Scrooge moves to the gravestone and reads his name upon it.

SCROOGE   Ebenezer Scrooge . . . Am I that man who died alone and friendless?

The finger points from the grave to him and back again.

SCROOGE   No, Spirit! Oh no, no!

The finger remains pointing at the headstone.

SCROOGE   Spirit! Hear me. I am not the man I was. I will not be the man I would have been without these ghostly visits. Why show me this if I am past all hope? Good Spirit, assure me that I yet may change these shadows you have shown me, by an altered life.

The ghost lowers his arm.

SCROOGE   I will honour Christmas in my heart, and try to keep it all the year. I will live in the Past, the Present, and the Future. The Spirits of all three shall strive within me. I will not shut out the lessons that they teach. Only, tell me that I may sponge away the writing on this stone!

A crack of thunder and a flash of lightning. Blackout.

49. The Carol Service

As mentioned in the introductory section, people are more open to coming to a church event during the Christmas period than at any other time of the year. We have already provided two ideas for events: a Christmas meal and a Christmas play. The other obvious events are the Nativity and the Carol Service. Ask yourself, 'Who am I trying to reach?' The answer will help you to define your Christmas strategy and determine your Christmas events.

The lunchtime Carol Service

The event

If you have a town-centre church or are based near a business area, consider holding a lunchtime Carol Service a couple of weeks before Christmas. The service should be short, approximately thirty minutes, and include well-known carols and a short lively message. Finish by inviting everyone to the other services and events to be held at your church over the Christmas period. The service should be followed with mince pies and tea/coffee or mulled wine. The church publicity stand, decorated for Christmas, should be erected near the queue for refreshments. Distribute the Christmas programme at the church door as people leave, maybe with a Christmas card, Christmas tract and a small Christmas gift.

If you don't have a church in a suitable venue, consider holding an open air Carol Service in the town centre. Advertise it in the same way and offer refreshments. You will also get passing shoppers stopping to join in.

The audience

Identify your likely guests. Are you in a town centre and likely to attract office and shop workers? Are you near the financial sector of a city and likely to attract 'professionals'? Maybe you are near an industrial estate and the guests will be manual labourers. Ensure that the type of service you hold fits the expected audience; consider carefully the Christmas message to deliver and the type of speaker most suitable. Also consider whether carols should be accompanied by the traditional organ or by more contemporary instruments.

The advertising

Ask local businesses and church members working in the area if they would put up posters advertising the service on their noticeboards. Also ask shops whether they would place a poster in their window. Make the posters colourful, attractive and eye-catching to ensure that they stand out among the glossy full-colour corporate posters on many business noticeboards. Include both the start and end time of the service on the poster, and keep to it – don't make people late back from lunch!

The candlelit Carol Service

The event

Most people love the atmosphere of the traditional candlelit Carol Service and would attend if invited. Singing carols learned in childhood in a darkly lit building decorated with evergreen trimmings and candles, smelling of pine and burning wax is a favourite way to get in the Christmas mood! This is a great opportunity for church members to invite unchurched family and friends. Encourage people to hold Christmas gatherings at their houses afterwards to eat

Christmas fare together, drink tea or mulled wine and socialize.

The audience

Friends, family, neighbours and the local community.

The advertising

Word of mouth. Invite friends and family. Advertise in the local press and with posters in local shop windows.

The Midnight Mass Carol Service

The event

We all know that drunken revellers joke about attending Midnight Mass on their way home from the pub on Christmas Eve; some even attempt it and end up slumped asleep or giggling at the back of the church. Have you ever considered holding a Midnight Service specifically aimed at this social group, aware of their condition and being prepared for it? Serve plenty of coffee and mince pies, accompanied by a band playing well-known carols in contemporary style, encouraging a sing-along. Attempting any type of ordered service may be a bad idea and the event should simply be an opportunity to introduce people to the church, make them aware of its existence and hand out invitations to events over the Christmas and New Year period. Church members should make themselves available to chat, so have a comfy counselling room available just in case! Also have church members on hand to give lifts home. If your church has a strong counselling section, maybe advertise the offer of a listening ear over the Christmas period.

The audience

Christmas revellers on their way home from Christmas Eve celebrations.

The advertising

Visit local pubs on a number of different evenings during December to sing carols and advertise the event; leave a poster with the landlord. Display a large advertisement on the church poster board for a couple of weeks beforehand to ensure that those who pass on their way home from a Saturday night out get a chance to see it.

The children's Carol Service

The event

This can be a Sunday morning Family Service. The children from groups attached to your church spend the weeks before the service learning carols and practising a Nativity play. Most people like to see a traditional Nativity, but those with children may prefer a different approach, having seen the same type of production year in, year out. Alternatively, you could host a Christmas puppet show in the service (see Idea 50).

The audience

Parents and siblings of those attending mothers and toddlers, linked nursery schools and Sunday school groups.

The advertising

Through the children's groups at your church, send a letter and tickets home with all children addressed to their parents/ guardians. Send six tickets per child, hoping they will also invite grandparents, and offer further tickets on request.

The joint youth Carol Service

The event

A highly contemporary, alternative Carol Service. Many young people have aspirations to become rock and pop stars, and there are many talented young people at church youth groups, many of whom also play in the church worship band. Join together with a number of other churches to host a 'Clash of the Carols' night with a large cash prize (e.g. £50). Contestants should pay £5 to enter and will be required to rework a carol, whether in thrash metal, Brit pop, rap, rock, pop, punk, soul style – it doesn't matter as long as the lyrics are faithful to the original! The evening should also include a short, snappy relevant message and a plug for the church youth groups, before announcing the winner. Run a tuck shop with Christmas sweets and mince pies available. The publicity boards for the church youth groups attending should be on display, with details of when they meet, what sort of activities they do and a pile of flyers detailing contact numbers and up and coming events.

You should have a list of entrants before the night, with band names, song titles and lengths. Ensure you have a fully working PA system and lights to create atmosphere.

The audience

Youth and students, predominantly fourteen- to twenty-five-year-olds.

The advertising

Display funky posters on school and college noticeboards. Youth group members should be encouraged to invite their friends to enter the contest or to come and watch them perform. Do a big push at a number of youth groups in your area. Advertise it with enough time for contestants to compose and practise; one month beforehand should be enough.

50. Puppet Show: 'Stable Relationships'

Many schools would welcome a presentation of the Christmas story in one of their assemblies near the end of term. Some puppet teams manage to tour their local primary schools over December, telling the Christmas story to thousands of children.

It is unlikely that you will be able to advertise your Christmas church services at state schools (*always* check first). However, you could follow up from the assembly with strategically timed leafleting to homes in the school's local community. Devise an identity for your puppet team: a memorable name and logo. Ask the school to introduce you in the assembly using the puppet team name, and have a large logo displayed either on the front of the puppet stage or on a board to one side. When you design your Christmas service invites, ensure that the name and logo can be clearly seen on the leaflets and identify yourself with the assembly puppet show (e.g. 'as seen in St Mary's and Heathfield primary schools').

Stable Relationships

A puppet play for six puppets © by Neil Simpson of the Chrestos Trust, with additional material by David Simpkin.

Cast

INNKEEPER: A battleaxe seaside landlady, abrupt and rude but not offensive

SIMEON:	Boy working in the inn, tells the story in flashback
JOSEPH:	Worried 'father'
MARY:	Pregnant with Jesus
SHEPHERD:	Stupid
WISE MAN:	Wise

Scene 1

Enter Simeon.

SIMEON

Hello! Welcome to the Crown of Thorns, the best pub in Jerusalem. I'm Simeon, landlord of the pub, and the best storyteller in town.

'Ere, I heard a great story in the bar last night. Apparently there was this Roman, this Greek, and this Samaritan and they were all . . . no . . . better not tell that story here. I'll tell you a story about what happened when I was much younger; that's much safer.

I was working in an inn in Bethlehem – you know, that little village about nine kilometres south of here? Yeah? I'd just got a job there . . . but now at this point we gotta tell the story as it happened. If this was on the telly, the screen would go all wavy and wobbly just to let you know we are going back in time – but you can't do that with a puppet stage so you'll just have to imagine it, OK? Start imagining it *now*!

Exit Simeon. Wavy music. Enter same Simeon puppet.

SIMEON

Hello! Simeon here. Did you recognize me? You know what I like about my job? You know what I like about working in an inn? Nothing. Absolutely nothing.

I've been working in this inn for two years now, and nothing ever happens. Well, I say nothing ever happens. I pour drinks, I make beds, I pour more drinks, I make more beds. Nothing exciting ever happens. When my dad got me this job I thought, 'Great! Working in a hotel in Bethlehem, I'll see all the stars – I'll see kings. It'll be great.' But not at our inn. We never get any stars staying here. Never had a king turn up. I'm not surprised, with our inn-keeper. Not exactly welcoming . . .

Voice off.

INNKEEPER	No! You can't have a room – we're full. In fact we're so full, even the beds can only stay one night!
SIMEON	Hear what I mean? We're never going to get any kings staying here.

Exit Simeon. Knock on door. Enter Innkeeper.

INNKEEPER	OK! I'll just open the door . . . Yes? What do you want?

Enter Joseph and Mary.

JOSEPH	We'd like a bed.
INNKEEPER	We don't sell them.

Door slam. Pause. Knock on door.

INNKEEPER	Yes? What do you want?
JOSEPH	Sorry, is this an inn?

INNKEEPER   No, it's a door. The inn is the building
                 around it.

Door slam. Pause. Knock on door.

INNKEEPER   Yes? What do you want?
JOSEPH   If this is an inn, do you have any rooms?
INNKEEPER   No.
JOSEPH   What? No rooms at all? Then where do all
                 the guests sleep?
INNKEEPER   In beds.

Door slam. Pause. Knock on door.

INNKEEPER   Yes? What do you want now?
JOSEPH   Can we stay at your inn?
INNKEEPER   We're full up.
JOSEPH   We're fed up.
INNKEEPER   We're packed out.
JOSEPH   We're left out.
INNKEEPER   I'm expecting guests.
MARY   I'm expecting a baby.
INNKEEPER   A baby? Well, where are you going to have it?
MARY   Well, that's what we're asking you . . .
INNKEEPER   Well . . . we've got a shed round the back.
JOSEPH   A shed? Is it safe?
INNKEEPER   Safe? It's safe.
MARY   Is it secure?
INNKEEPER   Secure? It's secure.
JOSEPH   Is it stable?
INNKEEPER   Stable? It *is* a stable.
MARY   We'll take it.
INNKEEPER   OK, but give it back when you've finished.

Exit Mary and Joseph.

INNKEEPER   Letting out that old stable – that should bring in some money! I wonder what else I could let out . . . The cellar! I'll get Simeon to clean the cellar. Simeon!

Enter Simeon.

SIMEON   Oops! Time I was off . . .

Chase music. Simeon and Innkeeper chase.

Scene 2

Enter Simeon.

SIMEON   Phew! Given her the slip. Clean out that old cellar? It would take me all year! No way!

Enter Mary.

SIMEON   Oh, hello. How are you settling in?
MARY   Fine, thanks.
SIMEON   Sorry to ask, but why were you going round looking for somewhere to stay when you are expecting a baby? Why weren't you at home, resting?
MARY   Well, we had to come here because of the census.
SIMEON   The what?
MARY   The census. The emperor wants to find out how many people there are in the empire, so he has made everybody go to their home town to be counted – that's why there are no rooms in any of the inns.
SIMEON   Oh. Hey! If everybody's got to go to their

	home town, well, you don't think we'll get somebody famous – a king or someone – do you?
MARY	Well, Gabriel told me . . .
SIMEON	Sorry? Who's Gabriel?
MARY	The angel.
SIMEON	Oh, right. Sorry, carry on . . .
MARY	Well, Gabriel told me . . .
SIMEON	An angel! This person is an angel! I mean, this angel is a person? I mean, I mean, an *angel*!
MARY	Yes, it was a bit of a surprise to me, as well. Anyway, Gabriel said that my baby was going to be a king for ever, King of the whole world, and not just the whole world, but King of everybody in it – and not just King of this world and everybody in it, but King of heaven as well!
SIMEON	Wow! You get no kings for ages, then three come along at once. A king being born here – now that is a surprise!
MARY	Not half as much of a surprise as it was to me. You see, he is God's baby, not Joseph's, so it was a bit difficult explaining it to Joseph. But Gabriel told him not to worry; it would be all right.

Voice off.

INNKEEPER	Simeon! I've got a little job for you . . .
SIMEON	Ooh! Must dash . . .

Exit Mary. Exit Simeon. Chase music. Simeon and Innkeeper chase.

Scene 3

Enter Innkeeper.

INNKEEPER   He must be somewhere! Where is that boy?

Knock on door. Door opens. Enter Shepherd. Sheep noises.

INNKEEPER   Are you a shepherd?
SHEPHERD   Yes. How did you know?
INNKEEPER   It was the sheep that gave it away.
SHEPHERD   What? They told you? Nah. Don't be silly. Sheep can't speak.
INNKEEPER   No, what I meant was the fact you seem to have a flock of sheep following you makes me think you might be a shepherd.
SHEPHERD   Oh, yeah.
INNKEEPER   Anyway, we don't let rooms to sheep.
SHEPHERD   That's all right! I didn't want a room.
INNKEEPER   Oh, what do you want then?
SHEPHERD   I'm looking for a baby.
INNKEEPER   We don't sell them. Simeon! Try and get rid of this stupid shepherd.

Exit Innkeeper. Enter Simeon.

SHEPHERD   I'm looking for a baby.
SIMEON   Can you remember where you last put him?
SHEPHERD   No, I don't mean I've lost a baby. I mean I haven't found a baby.
SIMEON   Hang on – you've not lost . . .? If you haven't lost him, there's no need to find him.
SHEPHERD   Yeah, but I haven't got him.
SIMEON   So you *have* lost him.
SHEPHERD   No, because I never had him in the first

place. Because I haven't got him, I'd have to find him before I could lose him – d'you see?

SIMEON   So you want to find this baby in order to lose him?

SHEPHERD   No, you're getting me confused now.

SIMEON   Well, join me and the rest of the audience then. We're already confused.

SHEPHERD   Look! I'm a shepherd. There I was, sitting in the field late at night, trying to work out how many sheep I had for the fifth time that night – it isn't easy counting sheep at night, you know.

SIMEON   No, you can't see in the dark, I suppose . . .

SHEPHERD   No! I kept falling asleep. Anyway, there I was counting my sheep, when suddenly there was this bright light, and lots of angels singing.

SIMEON   Well, at least you'd be able to see the sheep then.

SHEPHERD   Oh yes, I saw them. I saw them running over the hill in fright! It isn't every night you see a heavenly choir of angels all bright and shining and stuff. I thought, 'Look at all those sheep, scared of a few angels!' Then I thought, 'Angels?' Then I thought, 'Aaaaaaah . . . angels!' But the angel was very understanding. He said, 'Don't panic!' and I said, 'Aaaaaaaah!' And he said, 'Don't panic!' and I said, 'Aaaaaaaah!' And he said, 'NO!' So I stopped panicking. Then he said he had good news for everybody in the whole world. He said that the Messiah had been born in Bethlehem as a baby!

SIMEON   Hold on! Hold on! The Messiah?

SHEPHERD   Yeah. That's what we Jews call him – the Messiah. Of course the Greeks call him the

	Christ. It means 'God's Chosen One'. He's the one we're expecting to come from God and put everything right.
SIMEON	Put everything right?
SHEPHERD	To put everything right between us and God. You see, we've all done things wrong and we've all messed up. We've done things which hurt God and things which he doesn't like. This Messiah . . .
SIMEON	The Christ?
SHEPHERD	Yes – the Christ – is going to put it all right with God so we can be friends with God again, like we were meant to be. He's going to take the mess we've made in our lives and clean it up – that's why the angels were so excited, and that's why they said it was good news for everybody!
SIMEON	This baby you're looking for, the Messiah, the one who's going to make things right between us and God?
SHEPHERD	Yes?
SIMEON	I think I know where you can find him! If you go round the back and look in the stable, you'll find a baby – that's him!

Voice off.

INNKEEPER	Simeon! How would you like to do a little job for me?
SIMEON	That cellar's my little job. Time I was off!

Exit Shepherd. Exit Simeon. Chase music. Simeon and Innkeeper chase.

Scene 4

Enter Innkeeper.

INNKEEPER   I know he's here somewhere.

Knock on door.

INNKEEPER   Hold on, I'm just coming.

Door creaks open.

INNKEEPER   Yes? Who are you?

WISE MAN   Well, I'm a wise man. My friends and I have come a long way to be here.

INNKEEPER   Well, now you're here, what do you want?

WISE MAN   We're looking for God.

INNKEEPER   God? Do you know his surname?

WISE MAN   Err, I don't think he needs one. He's just God, isn't he?

INNKEEPER   Hold on, I'll just look in the hotel register . . . Lord Lucan, Glenn Miller, the crew of the *Marie Celeste*. No, no . . . we definitely haven't got anyone called God staying here.

WISE MAN   Are you sure?

INNKEEPER   Hold on. We are talking about *the* God, aren't we? You know, made the whole universe, tells the sun when to get up in the morning, keeps the stars in their place, knows everything – even the number of hairs on your head – causes it to rain or snow or stay dry . . . that God?

WISE MAN   Yes.

INNKEEPER   Well, I don't remember letting a room to anyone like that. I think I might just have recognized God if he came here and booked a room, don't you think? Tell you what, I'll ask round the other hotels, and if anyone else just happens to have the Supreme Being of the Universe renting a bed and breakfast in a tiny town like Bethlehem, I'll let you know.

WISE MAN   Oh, thanks.

INNKEEPER   Just don't hold your breath. God? Renting a room in an inn? How stupid can you get? Calls himself a wise man . . .

Exit Innkeeper. Enter Simeon.

SIMEON   'Scuse me. I couldn't help overhearing. You're looking for God?

WISE MAN   Yes.

SIMEON   I think I know where he is. I've just heard about the Christ, the one who's going to clean up the mess we've made in our lives – you know, all the lies and nasty words and nasty thoughts and all the bad things we do. Do you think the Christ actually IS God himself?

WISE MAN   Well, he might be. And you know where he is?

SIMEON   Yes!

WISE MAN   Oh, wonderful! Lead on! I expect someone as important as him will be in the penthouse suite – you know, the best room in the house.

SIMEON   Well . . . actually, he's round the back.

WISE MAN   Oh, a special apartment all to himself!

SIMEON   Well . . . actually, he . . . he's sharing it.

WISE MAN   Sharing it? Who with?

SIMEON   Three donkeys, five cows, fourteen chickens, and a couple of sheep.

WISE MAN   A load of animals!? Don't they make rather a mess of the carpet?

SIMEON   Silly! You don't get carpet in a stable.

WISE MAN   A stable?

SIMEON   Well, you didn't think we'd put the animals in one of the rooms, did you?

WISE MAN   No. But I didn't think you'd put God in the stable, either.

SIMEON   That's the only place we could find for him to be born as a man.

WISE MAN   But why did he allow it? Couldn't he have given himself the best room in the house? After all, he is God, so he can do anything. Why be born in a stable?

SIMEON   Well, I suppose no one can say he doesn't know what it's like to be poor or homeless or cold. Perhaps this way he's showing he understands what it's like to be a human.

WISE MAN   God becoming a human and living through all the pain and hurt and joy and fun – becoming just like us. What a wonderful thing for God to do! Perhaps that's part of how he's going to start clearing up the mess in our lives.

Voice over.

INNKEEPER   Simeon! I've got an incey wincey job for you to do!

SIMEON   Oh no! The cellar!

Exit Wise Man. Exit Simeon. Chase music. Simeon and Innkeeper chase.

Scene 5

Enter Simeon.

SIMEON   Right! You know that wavy stuff we did at the beginning; the stuff that means we're telling the story in the past? Well, we've got to do it again, only this time to tell you I'm telling it now. Right! Cue wavy music!

Exit Simeon. Wavy music. Enter same Simeon puppet.

SIMEON   Hi, it's me again, only this time I'm much older. You know, I look in the mirror and I think, 'Simeon, you haven't changed a bit!' Anyway, where was I?

Oh yeah, I'd just told you the story of Jesus being born in Bethlehem. I never did clean out that cellar, you know! But when he grew up, Jesus went round telling people how they needed to clean up their lives and stop doing the things that God didn't like and start doing the things that please God. Of course, that didn't please everybody, and when he was older, he was killed on a cross. His friends all thought it was a disaster – but then he rose from the dead three days later and proved that he was God.

His friends were saying that he'd taken the punishment for all the wrong things we've done, and forgiven us so that we can be friends with God.

And that is the story of Christmas.

Anyway, I can't stop here yakking all day – I've got an inn to run!

Exit Simeon. (Off-stage voice as Simeon exits.)

> Nathaniel! Nathaniel! I have a little job for
> you! Now where is that boy? He's never there
> when you want him!

50 Seasonal Sketches

by Neil Pugmire

This book includes sketches to be performed throughout the church's year, as well as on special occasions such as weddings, baptisms, school assemblies and church anniversaries. There are monologues, duologues, funny sketches, moving mimes and even a one-act play.

'An invaluable resource for the church at this time.'

David McInnes

NEIL PUGMIRE has been writing drama for 15 years for a variety of churches, schools and missions. He is artistic director of Top Cat Theatre Company in Portsmouth.